James Skinovsky
Sérgio Roll

Surgery by Minimally Invasive Biological Technologies

James Skinovsky
Sérgio Roll

Surgery by Minimal Access and New Surgical Technologies

The Amazing New Surgical World

LAP LAMBERT Academic Publishing

Impressum/Imprint (nur für Deutschland/only for Germany)
Bibliografische Information der Deutschen Nationalbibliothek: Die Deutsche Nationalbibliothek verzeichnet diese Publikation in der Deutschen Nationalbibliografie; detaillierte bibliografische Daten sind im Internet über http://dnb.d-nb.de abrufbar.
Alle in diesem Buch genannten Marken und Produktnamen unterliegen warenzeichen-, marken- oder patentrechtlichem Schutz bzw. sind Warenzeichen oder eingetragene Warenzeichen der jeweiligen Inhaber. Die Wiedergabe von Marken, Produktnamen, Gebrauchsnamen, Handelsnamen, Warenbezeichnungen u.s.w. in diesem Werk berechtigt auch ohne besondere Kennzeichnung nicht zu der Annahme, dass solche Namen im Sinne der Warenzeichen- und Markenschutzgesetzgebung als frei zu betrachten wären und daher von jedermann benutzt werden dürften.

Coverbild: www.ingimage.com

Verlag: LAP LAMBERT Academic Publishing GmbH & Co. KG
Heinrich-Böcking-Str. 6-8, 66121 Saarbrücken, Deutschland
Telefon +49 681 3720-310, Telefax +49 681 3720-3109
Email: info@lap-publishing.com

Herstellung in Deutschland:
Schaltungsdienst Lange o.H.G., Berlin
Books on Demand GmbH, Norderstedt
Reha GmbH, Saarbrücken
Amazon Distribution GmbH, Leipzig
ISBN: 978-3-8465-8779-9

Imprint (only for USA, GB)
Bibliographic information published by the Deutsche Nationalbibliothek: The Deutsche Nationalbibliothek lists this publication in the Deutsche Nationalbibliografie; detailed bibliographic data are available in the Internet at http://dnb.d-nb.de.
Any brand names and product names mentioned in this book are subject to trademark, brand or patent protection and are trademarks or registered trademarks of their respective holders. The use of brand names, product names, common names, trade names, product descriptions etc. even without a particular marking in this works is in no way to be construed to mean that such names may be regarded as unrestricted in respect of trademark and brand protection legislation and could thus be used by anyone.

Cover image: www.ingimage.com

Publisher: LAP LAMBERT Academic Publishing GmbH & Co. KG
Heinrich-Böcking-Str. 6-8, 66121 Saarbrücken, Germany
Phone +49 681 3720-310, Fax +49 681 3720-3109
Email: info@lap-publishing.com

Printed in the U.S.A.
Printed in the U.K. by (see last page)
ISBN: 978-3-8465-8779-9

SUMMARY

1

To my dear parents Leiba and Mathilde Skinovsky , from the other side continue to light my way in this existence;

To my beloved wife and children Giannini, Lucas and Thiago, source of energy and inspiration;

To my dear brother and sisters Luiz, Rosane and Rejane, who prepared shortcuts to our evolutionary track

To colleagues who have lent their knowledge to enhance this work, speccialy my dear firend and master Dr Sérgio Roll, pioneer of videosurgery!

MAIN AUTHORS

JAMES SKINOVSKY, PhD

Chairman Professor, Surgery Department, Positivo University Medical School, Curitiba – Brazil

Head of Surgery Department, Red Cross University Hospital, Curitiba – Brazil

Head of LapSurg International Institute of Endoscopic Surgery

SÉRGIO ROLL, PhD

President of the American Hernia Society
Professor, Post-Graduate Department, Positivo University, Curitiba – Brazil

COLABORATORS

ALCIDES JOSÉ BRANCO FILHO, MD

Surgical Staff, Red Cross University Hospital, Curitiba – Brazil

ALMINO CARDOSO RAMOS, MD

Head of Gastro Obeso Medical Center, São Paulo – Brazil

ANDRÉ VICENTE BIGOLIN

Medical student, Luteran University of Brazil (ULBRA), Canoas – Brazil

ANÍBAL WOOD BRANCO, MD

Urology Staff - Red Cross University Hospital, Curitiba – Brazil

FERNANDA KEIKO TSUMANUMA

Surgery Staff, Red Cross University Hospital, Curitiba – Brazil

FERNANDO CREBS CIRNE LIMA, MD

Head of 10th Enfermary, Santa Casa Hospital, Porto Alegre – Brazil

FRANCISCO EMANUEL ALMEIDA

Surgery Resident, Red Cross University Hospital, Curitiba – Brazil

FLÁVIO AUGUSTO MARTINS FERNANDES JR, MD

Specialist in Endoscopic Surgery by Pernambuco University, Recife – Brazil

GIOVANNI DAPRI, PhD

Assistent Surgery Professor, Gastrointestinal Surgery Department

European School of Laparoscopic Surgery

Saint-Pierre University Hospital

Brussels, Belgium

GUSTAVO CARVALHO, PhD

PhD by Keio University, Japan

Surgery Professor, Pernambuco Federal University, Recife - Brazil

ELSA (Board of Governors Member), SAGES and ALACE

JEFFREY M. MARKS, PhD

Associate Professor, Surgery Department

Director of Endoscopic Surgery

University Hospitals, Case Western Reserve University School of Medicine, Cleveland, USA

JOSEMBERG CAMPOS, PhD

Head of Neogastro, Recife and Director of Gastro Obeso Medical Center, São Paulo – Brazil

LEANDRO TOTTI CAVAZZOLA, PhD

Post-Doctoral in Minimally Invasive Surgery and NOTES - Case Western Reserve University, Cleveland, Ohio, USA

Associate Professor, Operative Technique, Luteran University of Brazil – Ulbra, Canoas - Brazil

Associate Anatomy Professor, Health Science Federal University and Rio Grande do Sul Federal University, Porto Alegre – Brazil

MARCUS VINÍCIUS DANTAS DE CAMPOS MARTINS, MD

Associate Surgery Professor, Estácio de Sa University, Rio de Janeiro – Brazil

Associate Editor Brazilian Journal of Videoendoscopic Surgery

MAURICIO CHIBATA, MD

Associate Surgery Professor, Positivo University Medical School, Curitiba – Brazil

MANOEL GALVÃO NETO, PhD

Coordenator Gastro Obeso Medical Center, São Paulo – Brazil

LUIZ ALBERTO DE CARLI, PhD

Head of General Surgery Service, 10 [th] Enfermary, Santa Casa Hospitals, Porto Alegre – Brazil

Coordenator – Teaching and Research Videosurgery Institute, Santa Casa Hospitals, Porto Alegre

MARCOS D. FERREIRA, PhD

Post-Doctoral Research Fellow in Robotic and Minimally Invasive Surgery, Harvard Medical School, USA

MARCOS TANG,MD

Surgery Instructor, 10 [th] Enfermary, Santa Casa Hospitals, Porto Alegre – Brazil

MIGUEL PRESTES NÁCUL, MD

Coordenator Videosurgery, Emergency Hospital, Porto Alegre - Brazil
Coordenator – Endoscopic Surgery Course, Parque Belém Hospital and
Teaching and Research Institute , Moinhos de Vento Hospital, Porto Alegre -
Brazil
Associate Editor Brazilian Journal of Videoendoscopic Surgery.

MARCO CEZÁRIO DE MELO, PhD

Head of Surgical Staff DIGEST and Head of Videosurgery Training
Center,Recife – Brazil
Associate Editor Brazilian Journal of Videoendoscopic Surgery

MÔNICA TESSMANN ZOMER, MD

Gynecologist – Red Cross University Hospital, Curitiba - Brazil

NICOLAS BOURDEL , MD

Gynecologist – Gynecologic Surgery Department, CHU Estaing, Clermont-
Ferrand, France

RAFAEL WILLIAM NODA, MD

Surgical and Endoscopy Staff – Red Cross University Hospital, Curitiba - Brazil

RICARDO ZUGAIB ABDALLA, PhD

Assistent Surgeon from Surgery II, Hospital das Clínicas, São Paulo University,
Brazil

Chairman Robotic Surgery, Sírio Libanês Hospital, São Paulo - Brazil

RICARDO ZORRÓN, PhD

Head of Surgery Department, Teresopolis School of Medicine, Rio de Janeiro – Brazil

Associate Professor, Strassbourg University, EITS-IRCAD, France

RICHARD SATAVA, PhD

Surgery Professor
University of Washington Medical Center
Seattle, Washington, USA

RODRIGO BISCUOLA GARCIA, MD

Surgery Staff, Sírio Libanês Hospital, São Paulo - Brazil

ROGERIO AUGUSTO PEIXER CAVALLIERE, MD

Surgery Staff, Red Cross University Hospital, Curitiba – Brazil

WILLIAM KONDO, MD

Gynecologist Red Cross University Hospital, Curitiba – Brazil

Ex-Fellow, Gynecologic Surgery Department, CHU Estaing, Clermont-Ferrand, France

From the advent of laparoscopy or Minimally Invasive Surgery (MIS), there have been continuous attempts to improve and enhance this extraordinary advance in the art and science of surgery. With the maturation of laparoscopic surgery, this revolutionary approach has become the "gold standard" in minimally invasive procedures, but new inventions and surgical approaches need to demonstrate a tangible improvement in patient care, especially especially in relation to their safety and satisfaction, but must also discuss the issues of ease of use and satisfactory conditions in cost-effectiveness relation. Together with the realization of this publication, there has been a series of challenges for the laparoscopic MIS approach, with the focus among these alternatives minilaparoscopy, robotic surgery, surgery by natural orifices (NOTES) and surgery by single access and its synonyms (such as SILS, Tues, spas, etc.).

In order to clarify the current state of the art based on these approaches, Professor James Skinovsky met a group of international experts to cast his critical eye not only for the variety of surgical approaches for the MIS, but also to explore the basic science and potential of future directions. But the great strength of this book is the documentation of clinical and technical variety. In this book are not present only the sampling of the wide variety of technical approaches previously mentioned, but also the clinical applications in general surgery (cholecystectomy, appendectomy, GERD, and bariatric surgery), gynecologic surgery and endoluminal surgery. A particularly valuable contribution is the chapter of Professor Ricardo Zorron, which brings critically important data from clinical studies, which can be used to emphasize the value of NOTES.

This book is a valuable introduction and compilation of the different procedures in practice today, but most important is a "instantaneous in time", which captures a unique period in the history of surgery, where the forces of creativity and invention are interacting to redefine who really understands the essence of the surgery. It shows not only the strengths and weaknesses of various techniques and applications in minimally invasive surgery, but also reveals the strengths and vulnerabilities underlying of these pioneers. Future generations of surgeons will be able to look back and understand not just the technology that led to this revolution, but also the intimate perception of the people who made it happen.

Richard M. Satava, USA

"The history of civilization is the story of building on what has was learned. It is the evolution from cuneiform writing on stone to the modern press and internet. It is the evolution of thought, science, art and technology always based on what our ancestors developed with great difficulty and effort"

Roberto Civita

It is undeniable the progress of medicine since Hippocrates removed it from the field of superstition to bring it to the light of science. It is notorious its evolution.

When we performed the first videolaparoscopic cholecystectomy in latin America, 1990, we could not predict that many of these videoendoscopic procedures become the "gold standard" in the daily practice of the surgeon in a short time. The size of the technical evolution of this approach was extraordinary and unprecedented in modern surgery.

As innovation continues, surgery in 21st century was increased by a technique of abdominal access using a single incision or portal.

Since the beginning, Professor Dr. James Skinovsky and his collaborators have been engaged in changing this paradigm. His effort to inform, train and enable surgeons in this new access via has been compensated by the involvement of other surgeons and certainly, this publication will provide an understanding of the concept, as well as the tools currently available to perform the technique.

A principle quickly developed by laparoscopic surgery was the concept of triangulation. This was necessary for adequate exposition of the operative field, while an ergonomically favorable position was maintained for the surgeon and assistants. Thus, the navel has emerged as a central location for many laparoscopic procedures.

It can be argued that this dogmatic principle would have been a limiting factor for many who thought of adopting this new conceptual idea in their surgical arsenal.

However, with the development of long or angled optics and new access portals and articulated instruments, surgeons began to familiarize themselves with the technique and found a new surgical ergonomics, which is equally appropriate or better than the one used since the beginning of laparoscopic surgery.

Moreover, the recent interest in endoluminal procedures and techniques through natural orifices, the new trend of using a single portal came in line with this technological revolution, as well as, quickly became fashionable and acceptable by patients.

Since the beginning of the development of this new technology and access via, a fundamental principle established was that of protecting patients and ensuring that the surgical resolution is the same ever achieved and well defined by laparoscopic surgery performed with multiple portals.

The zeal and ability of Dr Skinovsky resulted in a study characterized by a clear exposition of all principles of this new technology, which will allow a rapid development of this new access via, assuring that good results are obtained.   After 22 years of the realization of the first videolaparoscopic cholecystectomy in the world, this book introduces readers to a new era in the field of surgery, offering everyone a great potential for the future.

This book reflects the effort and dedication of the editors who succeeded in bringing together a multidisciplinary group of talented surgeons committed to the disclosure of the method and knowledge.

It was an immense pleasure and an honor to present this publication, which will be subject to mandatory consultation to all who wish to update on the subject.

I want everyone to benefit from the pages that open the following.

Sergio Roll, Brazil

SURGERY BY MINIMAL ACCESS (SMA)

James Skinovsky

Sérgio Roll

INTRODUCTION

The year of 1987 marked the beginning of videosurgery, representing a complete change in the paradigm lived and taught until then, in the global surgical field. The trauma and pathophysiological changes caused by surgical procedures suffered remarkable regression, resulting in less pain and faster return to labor and more satisfactory cosmetic results.

The fast and continuous improvement of the optical system, as well as the instrumental used in videosurgery, have allowed that more complex procedures could be performed by this approach. In the beginning, acute stages of surgical diseases such as acute cholecystitis, were cited as prohibitive for videolaparoscopic resolution, as well as neoplasic pathologies. One by one the barriers to the so-called minimally invasive surgery are being torn down, until in modern times major operations like gastroduodenopancreatectomy are performed safely by this method.

The emergence of videosurgery and of the parallel related technological development, new equipment and approaches have emerged and are being tested around the world.

All the new medical technology - surgery must respond in its precocious stage of use, the three questions that should guide the continuity or not of its employment:

• Is it feasible?

• Is it safe?

• Worth it?

All approaches which now remain under the umbrella of the sma –
Surgery by Minimal Access, as NOTES (Natural Orifice Translumenal
Endoscopic Surgery), Minilaparoscopy and Laparoendoscopic Single Site
Surgery (LESS), at this time, are trying to answer these questions.

NEW APPROACHES AND SURGICAL TECHNOLOGIES

The massive investment in technology has allowed the effective
development of surgery in the interior of hollow organs, called endomuminal
surgery, as well as the NOTES[1]. This last approach still needs to overcome
some barriers, so that in times to come can become an effective option for daily
clinical and surgical application. Even if in the future this method cannot be
routinely applied in the manner classically proposed, the stupendous evolution
of endoscopic devices, as well as the instrumental correlate has increased
greatly the arsenal for endoluminal surgery, ranging from the removal of
submucosal tumors of the upper and/or lower gastrointestinal tract until the
bariatric surgeries performed by intragastric via that still crawl, but that will
certainly be their place according to technological development.

The evolution of super-fast internet has allowed the dream still precocius
of performing surgeries at a distance (telesurgery), already performed in a
precocious way, but that may in future allow access for patients in poor and
isolated communities to the surgical procedures necessary and unattainable so
far, be the distance and/or economic issues.

Robotic surgery is a reality, but still cannot be effected in a ordinary way
around the world due to its cost and technical complexity, but all technologies
began this way and, in its time, costs have been reduced and the manipulation
of its technology facilitated by simplification. This was true with the telephone,
the automobile and, more recently, with the computer.

Virtual reality, already used for decades to train pilots, maintains the
same reasoning. Several studies have demonstrated its guaranteed place in

medical education and surgical education, especially in relation to the teaching of new videosurgical technology [2,3,4,5,6,7].

Surgery by Single Access or LESS, with its several nominal variants emerged as an alternative to NOTES, one input device or more than a trocar inserted through a single incision is performed, where specialized instrumental is positioned to the proposed perform. Several surgical methods are being performed by this approach, from cholecystectomy to bariatric surgery[9,10].

The so-called Minilaparoscopy or Needlescopy also is finding its place in the surgical arsenal. The use of instrumental of smaller radius brings the consequent lower trauma, for both the abdominal wall and internal organs, leading to the metabolic consequences previously mentioned. Large surgical series, especially with respect to minilaparoscopic cholecystectomy, are already available in the literature[11,12].

All surgical procedures reported earlier: NOTES, LESS , Minilaparoscopy and Robotic Surgery has similar characteristics as the slightest trauma and minimal pathophysiological changes and they all can be characterized in the jargon "surgery with minimal scar" (scarless surgery). Because of the potential benefits common to these approaches, all can be fitted in the terminology Surgery by Minimal Access (SMA), bringing them together in a single terminology, because they are self-complementary, mixing concepts and approaches with a single goal, the benefit of patients.

The methods and instruments can be mixed according to the procedure and the stage of disease. The possibility of combined use of several instrumental technologies, are articulated distally, rigid and/or flexible, open a very large range of opportunities, allowing the right choice for each patient, unique in their anatomy and their disease.

The future development of NOTES procedures will eventually complete this integration, leading to the true performance of hybrid surgeries, when multi-channel portals will be used for single access, aided by portals and instrumental of 2 mm and, when necessary, assisted by endoscope and special instruments through natural orifices .

We cannot forget that, all this, will soon be aggregated to

nanotechnology, with directed endoscopic capsules and mini-robots, facilitating diagnosis and treatment by Minimal Access.

FINAL COMMENTS

It doesn't matter if the surgeon will perform the procedures using NOTES, LESS or Minilaparoscopy, in a pure or hybrid way. What matters is that the SMA is part of a large surgical arsenal, which begins by opencast surgery, passing by classic videosurgery and going until the advanced technology, perhaps in the future without any visible scar on the outside of the human body. Each patient is unique, as well as their disease. It depends on the surgeon to determine what is the best therapeutic choice to achieve a better mix of cosmetic results and safe and effective results of operations.

REFERENCES

1. Kalloo A, Singh VK, Jagannath SB, et al. Flexible transgastric peritoneoscopy: a novel approach to diagnostic and therapeutic interventions in the peritoneal cavity. Gastrointest Endosc 2004; 60(1):114–7.

2. Satava RM. Robotics, telepresence and virtual reality: a critical analysis of the future of surgery. Minimally Invasive Therapy. 1992;1:357-63.

3. Soler L, Ayach N, Nicolau S, Pennec X, Forest C, Delingette H, Mutter D, Marescoux J. Virtual reality, augmented reality and robotics in digestive surgery. World Scientific Publisher Edition. 2004; pp476-484.

4. Raibert M, PlayterR, Krummel,TM. The use of a virtual reality haptic device in surgical training. Acad Med.1998;73:596-97.

5. Ota D, Loftin B, Saito T, Lea R, Keller J. Virtual reality in surgical education. Comput Bio Med.1995; 25(2):127-137.

6. Ahlberg G, Heikkinen T, Leijonmarck CE, Rutqvist J, Arvidsson D. Does training in a virtual reality simulator improve surgical performance? Surg Endosc.2002;16(1):126-129.

7. Grantcharov TP, Rosenberg J, Pahle E, Funch-Jensen P. Virtual reality computer simulation. Surg Endosc.2001;15(3):242-244.

8. Kallo NA, Sibgh VK, Jagannath SB, Niiyama H, Vaugh CA, Magee CA, Kantsevoy SV. Flexible transgastric peritoneoscopy: a novel approach to diagnostic and therapeutic interventions. Gastrointest Endosc 2004; 60: 114-7.

9. Martins MVD, Skinovsky J, Coelho DE, Ramos A, Galvão Neto MP, Rodrigues J, de Carli L, Cavazolla, LT, Campos J, Thuller F, Brunetti A. Cholecystectomy by single trocar access – SITRACC: The first multicenter study. Surg Innov 2009;Dez – on line - sri.sagepub.com.

10. Saber AA, Elgamal MH, Itawi EA, Rao AJ. Single incision laparoscopic sleeve gastrectomy (SILS): a novel technique. Obes Surg 2008; 18:1338-1342.

11. Carvalho G.L., Silva F.W., Cavalcanti C.H., Albuquerque P.P.C., Araújo D.G., Vilaça T.G., Lacerda C.M. Colecistectomia Minilaparoscópicasem Utilização De Endoclipes: Técnica E Resultados Em 719 Casos. Rev Bras Videocir 2007;5(1):5-11

NOTES - CLINICAL EXPERIENCE AND FUTURE PROSPECTS

Ricardo Zorron

THE EVOLUTION OF THE NOTES CONCEPT

From 2007, NOTES applications (Natural Orifice Translumenal Endoscopic Surgery) in humans have been increasingly reported in the literature, although the beginning was slow due to the concentration of research on the transgastric access before other possibilities, the difficulty of obtaining approval by the Ethics in Research Committees and the lack of specific technology for flexible surgery. Since 2004, after the fundamental successful experimental study of Apollo Group, ALONG with presentations of Rao and Reddy of clinical casuistry in scientific meetings, there was a stimulus for research around the world toward a change of surgical paradigm [1,2], bringing curiosity and the surgical community a glimpse of the future of surgery.

The concept of NOTES surgery represents the evolution to the goal of less invasive procedures and new endoscopic approaches can demonstrate feasibility and safety, even for transgastric, colonic, urethral or vaginal access. The concept of NOTES began by the evolution of more invasive endoscopic procedures in recent years. Precursor of the concept of surgery by natural orifice were undoubtedly the performance of the more advanced invasive endoscopists and surgeons, with the evolution of endoscopic retrograde cholangiopancreatography (ERCP), percutaneous endoscopic gastrostomy (PEG), drainage of pancreatic pseudocysts, transanally endoscopic microsurgery (TEM), mucosal endoscopic resection (MER) for gastric and colonic cancer and interventional endoscopy. Moreover, the extraction of larger specimens by transorificial via were reported in laparoscopic surgery since 1993 [3-5]. Seifert, in 2000, reported transgastric endoscopic debridement in pancreatic necrosis in three patients with a Dormia basket, and also the removal of the necrotic spleen in one of these patients[6].

The growing enthusiasm in the medical community led to the formation of the NOSCAR working group (Natural Orifice Surgery Consortium for Assessment and Research) in 2006. The group, formed by a team of gastroenterologists and surgeons who represents the two companies ASGE

(American Society for Gastrointestinal Endoscopy) and SAGES (Society of American Gastrointestinal Endoscopic Surgeons). The main responsibility was to oversee the development of this field for clinical applications in humans of a careful and scientific way with a few avoidable mistakes. The result of the discussions was published as a White Paper and the International Conference about NOTES was held every year since 2005 [7].

The registry of NOSCAR about the human casuistry in NOTES in the U.S. began in 2008 with the support of both local societies. To avoid complications in the initial applications in humans, the group suggested questions to be solved for safe introduction of new techniques. Nevertheless, these recommendations apply primarily the indicated transgastric access, not taking into account that most creative international groups have advanced on the safer transvaginal via, using equipment available [8-14].

I Important experimental woks were initiated in studies on the physiology of surgery by natural orifices, infection, visualization and guidance. Entry and safe closure of the visceral wound were the technical key researches performed by surgeons and technicians in the industry to allow NOTES surgery. In the following year, around the world research overcame problems with creativity, instead of new technologies, using the vaginal approach (dispensing technology for opening and closure), and the use of adaptation of available instruments. However, the learning curve of flexible surgery in the experimental training has frustrated many researchers, leading them to concentrate efforts to the easier path of umbilical laparoscopy or surgery by single portal (Single Port Surgery). So far there are 256 human cases of NOTES published in the literature since 2007, and over 362 cases as preliminary results of the IMTN[15] (International Multicenter Clinical Trial on NOTES) study, a multiinstitutional international register initiated by the Brazilian NOTES Research Group, resulting in a casuistry of 617 cases listed in **Table 1**.

Table.1. Human casuistry in NOTES available in the literature. ND = not documented.

Study	#cases	Procedure	Complications (N,%)	OP Time (min)	Postoperative Stay (hours)
NOTES TRANSVAGINAL					
Branco et al (2007)	1	TV Cholecystectomy	0	150	24
Bessler et al (2007)	1	TV Cholecystectomy	0	210	24
Marescaux et al (2007)	1	TV Cholecystectomy	0	180	48
Zornig et al (2007)	1	TV Cholecystectomy	0	85	
Zorron et al (2007)	1	TV Cholecystectomy	0	66	48
Zorron et al (2008)	4	TV Cholecystectomy	0	45-115	48
Ramos A et al (2008)	32	TV Cholecystectomy	0	38	6
Branco AW et al (2008)	1	TV Nephrectomy	0	170	12
Zorron et al (2008)	1	TV Cancer Staging	0	105	48
DeCarli L et al (2008)	1	TV Cholecystectomy	1/1	85	72
Forgione et al (2008)	3	TV Cholecystectomy	0	136	48
Noguera et al (2009)	15	TV Cholecystectomy	1/15	89.62	12-24
DeCarli L et al (2009)	12	TV Cholecystectomy		125.8	48
Gumbs et al (2009)	4	TV Cholecystectomy	0	209	23
Davila et al (2009)	1	TV Cholecystectomy	0	ND	24
Sousa et al (2009)	4	TV Cholecystectomy	0	210	24
Zornig et al (2009)	68	TV Cholecystectomy	1/51	51	48-144
Palanivelu et al (2009)	8	TV Cholecystectomy	1/8	148.5	96
IMTN Multicenter Study Group (2009)	362	TV Cholecystectomy TV Appendectomy TV Sleeve Gastrect TV Nephrectomy TV Colectomy TG Appendectomy TG Cholecystectomy	32/362	99-111	45.01
Palanivelu et al (2008)	1	TV Appendectomy	0	103.5	48
Bernhardt et al (2008)	1	TV Appendectomy	0	ND	72
Lacy et al (2008)	1	TV Colectomy	0	150	96
Burghardt et al (2008)	1	TV Colectomy	0	ND	ND
Ramos et al (2008)	4	TV Sleeve Gastrect	0	95	48
Fischer et al (2009)	1	TV Sleeve Gastrect	0	ND	ND
Zorron et al (2009)	1	TV Retroperitoneoscopy	1/1	210	96
TRANSGASTRIC NOTES					
Rao & Reddy (2005)	14	TG Appendectomy TG Tubal Ligation TG Cholecystectomy TV Cholecystectomy	2/14	ND	ND
Marks et al (2007)	1	TG PEG Rescue	0	ND	ND
Hazey et al (2008)	10	TG Cancer Staging	2/10	ND	ND
Horgan et al (2009)	11	TG Appendectomy TV Cholecystectomy	0	78-165	24-48
Dallemagne et al (2009)	5	TG Cholecystectomy	0	150	ND
Auyiang et al (2009)	4	TG Cholecystectomy	0	ND	ND
Salinas et al (2009)	39	TG Cholecystectomy TV Cholecystectomy	18/39	140	8.2
TRANSVESICAL NOTES					
Gettman et al (2007)	1	TU Peritoneoscopy	0	40	24
NOTES TRANSCOLÔNICO					
Zorron et al (2009)	1	TC Colectomy	0	350	144
TOTAL	617	-	59 (9.6%)	-	-

DEVELOPMENT OF CLINICAL APPLICATIONS

TRANSVAGINAL NOTES (TV):

By far the most performed NOTES access, transvaginal abdominal surgery represents a true application of the possibly safer of the new methods. Different from transgastric and transcolonic access, transvaginal approach has a long history of routine treatments by the access in gynecological interventions. Konrad Langenbeck performed the first transvaginal hysterectomy in 1813; in 1901, Dimitri von Ott described for the first time the peritoneoscopy through colpotomy. Years later, in 1942, Albert Decker invented what is known as the Decker Culdoscope, performing transvaginal procedures with regular environment air[16,17]. Bueno reported in 1949, the first successful case of incidental vaginal appendectomy during vaginal hysterectomy, and now many operations have been described for transvaginal open surgery, including a larger number of appendicectomy[18,19]. Using a hybrid procedure, Tsin and cols published vaginal cholecystectomy and others simultaneous operations after a vaginal hysterectomy with a trocar, formal laparoscopic instruments through the anterior abdominal wall, calling the technique as "Culdolaparoscopy"[20]. These studies using surgery by vaginal access (potentially contaminated) to perform abdominal procedures (sterile) had low rates of infectious complications. Apparently, access may represents no risk to the fertility of patients in most series, for now, the transvaginal culdoscopy method is also often indicated for the investigation of infertility of pelvic origin. However, most series still avoid the procedure in nulliparous.

NOTES Cholecystectomy by transvaginal via in human cases were performed by different groups of pioneers in 2007. Zorrón and cols [8,9], Branco and cols [10], Marescaux and cols [11] and Bessler and cols [14] performed hybrid NOTES using an umbilical needle or trocar to obtain liver retraction, and using flexible endoscopic instruments to perform dissection, clipping in the initial casuistry. Zornig and cols [12] described transvaginal cholecystectomy using a combination of rigid transvaginal laparoscopic camera and retraction by a long transvaginal trocar, and a 5 mm umbilical trocar, using this last one to perform the dissection, clipping and cutting. With more experience, most groups have abandoned the practice of using endoscopic clips, preferring to install clips either by endovaginal via with long laparoscopic clippers, or resorting to more hybrid procedures through an umbilical trocar.

The use of laparoscopic assistance in NOTES clearly represents a hybrid procedure, but it shortened operative time and allowed the improvement of safety, retraction and visualization. The deficiency in technology of appropriate tools can also be overcome through the use of hybrid techniques, and represents an alternative to start the learning curve for flexible surgery.

Other groups that performed clinical trials about transvaginal NOTES are using hybrid processes as a step to a safer and faster transition to NOTES [21-33]. The concept of "Totally NOTES" was reached in 2009 by Sousa and cols [26], using two flexible endovaginal endoscopes by Gumbs and cols[27] and Davila and cols[28], using only rigid instruments and flexible endoscope by transvaginal via.

The concept of pure NOTES also with the use of the flexible endoscope was first applied by the transvaginal appendicectomy by Palanivelu and cols[29], and later by Bernhardt and cols[30]. Lacy and cols[31] described the first case of transvaginal hybrid sigmoidectomy in a patient with sigmoid colon cancer using a combination of transvaginal rigid instrumentation and minilaparoscopic instruments, naming the technique as MA-NOS. Burghardt and cols[32] applied transvaginal NOTES to the right colectomy.

The advantages of using a combination of the piece extraction by transvaginal via is evident, and more voluminous colorectal specimens can be properly extracted by this via. However, these groups have also seen that the future way can be in use of transcolonic NOTES in colorectal surgery, which could contribute significantly to avoid auxiliary incisions in both sexes, with a clear evolution of minimally invasive colorectal surgery.

Ramos and Galvão, from the Gastrobeso Center group in São Paulo presented a first series of Sleeve Gastrectomy by transvaginal NOTES [33] (Figure 1). Four patients were submitted to the technique using flexible

25

transvaginal visualization, dissection and extraction combined with transumbilical stapling, recognizing the limitation of the size and shape of stapplers and instruments to allow the full use of vaginal via, instead of umbilical assistance. Fischer and cols described a case using similar technique[34].

Figure 1 Transvaginal Sleeve Gastrectomy - detail of the vaginal extraction of large specimen. (courtesy Ramos and cols, Gastrobeso Center, Sao Paulo, Brazil)

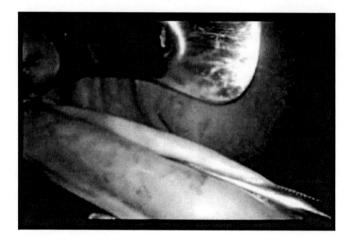

In most cases, a direct transvaginal access can be achieved by simple dissection of the posterior vaginal fornix. The initial umbilical laparoscopic visualization is used after the peritoneal insufflation by many groups to initially install a vaginal trocar and using rigid or flexible vaginal camera. The closure of the vaginal wound is not a problem of the approach, and it is performed under direct vision externally with absorbable wires by conventional instruments. The approaches by transvaginal NOTES have less potential for complications such as peritonitis and fistula than the others translumenals access [34]. Potential disadvantages of transvaginal surgery are the necessary use of antibiotics and bladder catheterization, the concern with dyspareunia and infertility, and with operative time longer than the formal laparoscopy.

TRANSGASTRIC NOTES:

The secure closure of the transgastric access still represents a problem for the published series, and most procedures could only be performed using laparoscopic assistance. The gastric access was performed under laparoscopic visualization, and the closure was performed using one or two laparoscopic trocars, or new technologies like G-Prox (USGI, San Clemente, CA), T-Tags (Ethicon, Cincinnati, OH), or Overstich (Apollo Endosurgery, Austin, TX).

The initial series of Rao and Reddy suggested the use of endoscopic clips to close the gastric access, but this concept was not followed by the following groups because it represents only the position of mucous membranes. The gastric access was historically used initially in human experimental series and before the transvaginal approach, for many reasons. As the surgeon with experience knows, the "hostile" pelvis because of previous adherences, pelvic infections and endometriosis are more common than a "hostile" superior abdomen, possibly making the transgastric access more attractive, especially for the general surgeon with experience in high digestive endoscopy. However, the extraction of voluminous specimens should not be solved through this via, since the esophagus allows only an instrumental in maximum diameter of about 2 cm. Reported complications in initial studies suggest that the use of the overtube in the esophagus can be beneficial to avoid bruising and lacerations. Until the present date, only seven groups clinically reported the transgastric surgery for cholecystectomy, appendectomy and staging of cancer with good results in small number of cases [1,25,36-40]. Rao and Reddy from India, described a human pioneer series initially applying flexible transgastric surgery for nine cases of appendicectomy and other applications1. Successful rescue of endoscopic gastrostomy (PEG) through this via was described by Marks and

27

cols[37], and of initial human application for staging of pancreatic cancer by transgastric via was also reported by Hazey and cols[38].

Horgan and cols reported a case of transgastric appendicectomy in 11 cases of NOTES in his publication using flexible hybrid endoscopy[25]. They recognized the need for the use of laparoscopic clips instead of endoscopic clips for security reasons, and, in this case, the gastric closure was tried with a new suture device (G-prox), but there was a need to reinforce laparoscopically the sutures. This was also the experience of Auyang and cols, in four cases of transgastric cholecystectomy, in which the gastrotomy was closed by intraluminal via, but laparoscopically resutured[40].D'Allemagne and cols, used the laparoscopic camera orientation for the opening of gastric access, and a combination of flexible dual-channel endoscopes and laparoscopic instruments in five patients [39]. The gastric closure was performed through interrupted suture using a 2 mm laparoscope and a needle holder of 3 mm placed side by side.

Salinas and cols from Lima, Peru, reported a series of 27 cases of transgastric NOTES cholecystectomy with laparoscopic assistance[36]. Different from last transgastric techniques described here, together with 12 cases by transvaginal via reported a rate of 20% of postoperative complications, including reoperations. They noticed that the complications were related to the learning curve, because the rate declined after the first year of experience.

Even so, the initial enthusiasm around the transgastric access was contained by the limitations of technology, which had a slow evolution for the surgical needs for safe gastric opening and closure, together with the limited space of instruments to work in the diameter of the esophagus, and the initial confused visualization and orientation, worsened by the need for spatial retroflexion to the superior abdomen. However, transgastric access still seems to have future possibilities, since it can be used in both sexes, and the development of more technology is expected (FIGURE 2).

Figure 2 Transgastric NOTES cholecystectomy - retroflected flexible visualization and use of laparoscopic assistance for the closure of the gastrostomy. (courtesy Galvao and cols, Gastrobeso Center, Sao Paulo, Brazil)

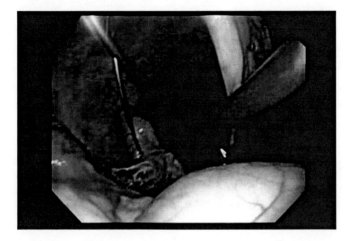

TRANSESOPHAGEAL (TE) AND TRANSVESICAL (TVES) NOTES:

Although the promising access suggested by the publication of experimental studies, clinical casuistry of thoracic transesophageal and mediastinal NOTES access for diagnosis and therapeutic has not been published. An innovative procedure to perform the treatment for achalasia was recently proposed and implemented by transmural flexible endoscopy.

The methods consist of a perforation of the mucosa of the lower esophagus, the confection of a protected submucosal tunnel and, finally, the endoscopic sphincterotomy of the circular fibers of the inferior esophageal sphincter. Presentations of abstracts at recent meetings reported human cases of the centers of Venezuela and Japan, with good initial results[41].

The performance of NOTES by transurethral via (transvesical) in animals have shown the possibilities for future applications, but only a human report has been registered so far. Gettman and Blute in 2007 reported the first case of transvesical peritoneoscopy with suprapubic cystostomy installation during robotic prostatectomy[42]. With the help of laparoscopic orientation, transvesical puncture and entrance into the peritoneal cavity was performed using a rigid cystoscope, followed by insertion of a flexible ureteroscope, being performed complete peritoneoscope. The resulting orifice was not closed, but occluded by the insertion of cystostomy tube.

Despite the lack of concern about infection and ease of access and closure, the main access problems were recognized for the transvesical access, a limitation of technology and the diameter of the workspace, making unfeasible the use of more robust instrumentation.

NOTES BY TRANSCOLONIC VIA (TC):

Transcolonic NOTES was the subject of few recent experimental studies, suggesting that access could be an attractive option for the treatment of diseases of the colon and abdominals[3-8]. *Transanally Endoscopic Microsurgery* (TEM), developed and described by Buesser and cols in the early '80s, it is currently a minimally invasive alternative for most benign lesions of the rectum and is a pioneering effort in the field of surgery through natural orifices[43].

However, as transgastric access, the advantages of using transcolonic access to target extra-colonic organs as gallbladder, stomach and others, would show little advantage, in relation to all potential risks involved.

Technical barriers such as the risk of infection, safe entrance into the abdominal cavity and secure closure of the colonic access made it difficult to indicate this via in the same period in which the clinical application of vaginal and transoral access was possible. Zorrón et cols in 2010 effectively developed new flexible techniques of joint studies of animal transcolonic, and a perirectal transcolonic access was designed to allow access and treatment in the abdominal and retroperitoneal cavity and used in human experience[44,45].

The technique developed by this group, and tested in animal model of survival rate, NOTES Perirectal Access (PNA), was used to start clinical applications. This study describes the transcolonic NOTES procedure for the

30

first time in literature, endoscopic using flexible instruments in a case of retossigmoidectomy and TME for rectal cancer.

In one patient with 54 years of age with a rectal adenocarcinoma, total resection of mesorectal and retossigmoidectomy with lymphadenectomy was performed using a posterior transcolonic access near the anal verge. The mesorectal dissection was achieved using a flexible colonoscope and endoscopic instrumentation and laparoscopic assistance. The specimen was extracted by transanal via and transorificial anastomosis was performed with proximal stoma **(Figs.4A-D).**

Fig. 5A. Transcolonic Retossigmoidectomy using Perirectal NOTES Access (PNA). A low entrance at the rectum allows the performance of anastomosis for cancer of the medium and superior rectum. Schematic of the mesorectal dissection by flexible endoscope. **Fig. 5B.** Endoscopic dissection for total mesorrectum excision. **Fig.5C.** Transcolonic extraction of the specimen. **Fig.5D.** Transrectal NOTES Retossigmoidectomy with TME using intra-retal Single Port. (courtesy Zorron and cols, Rio de Janeiro, Brazil)

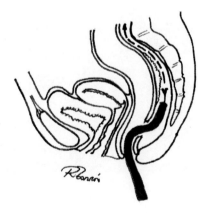

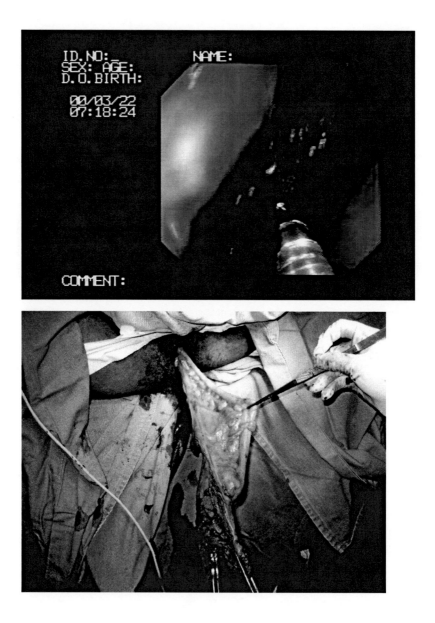

Certainly, transrectal access raises concerns for infection control and still requires the need for secure closure of the colon. However, a low entry point, as described in this study, using a retroperitoneal tunnel instead of puncturing the rectosigmoid junction, previous closure of the proximal rectum, allowed a relatively isolated field that can be adequately disinfected, thus avoiding the intestinal preparation. Despite the need for a colorectal perforation, the choice of the entry point into the exact line of the anastomosis minimizes the fear of unnecessary viscerotomy.

NOTES SPECIAL APPLICATIONS
CANCER STAGING

Previous clinical work about the use of surgery by natural orifices for cancer was described by Hazey and cols using a transgastric access to evaluate the resectability of pancreatic cancer[38], Zorrón and cols through the transvaginal via to perform biopsies of the liver, peritoneum, greater omentum and ovarian to evaluate carcinomatosis[46] (Figures 6 A-6B). In the first, a transgastric NOTES evaluation showed accuracy in staging in 9 of 10 patients. Determination of resectability was determined based on the laparoscopic diagnosis and through transgastric NOTES by examiners independent of each other, and showed the feasibility of exploration of the transgastric endoscopic cavity. In the current small casuistry about NOTES for surgery of cancer, tumor implantation hasn't been described, but it is a matter of concern in ontological resections.

Fig. 6A. Staging of abdominal cancer thorugh transvaginal NOTES via with flexible endoscope. Biopsy of diaphragm. Fig. 6B. Hepatic biopsy transvaginal NOTES.

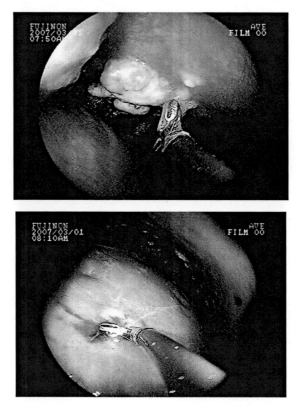

RETROPERITONEAL AND UROLOGICAL SURGERY

The transvesical, transvaginal, and transcolonic access has been defended by the experimental investigation as being more appropriate for access the superior abdominal to the structures that could be more difficult to work with the use of a transgastric procedure. In 2007, Branco and cols performed a transvaginal nephrectomy by hybrid NOTES using the endoscope through the vaginal access and two additional of 5 mm in the abdomen [47]

34

(Figure 6). The patient had postoperative without intercurrences and was discharged 12 hours after the procedure.

Also in 2007, Gettman and Blute described transvesical peritoneoscope using rigid and flexible standard tools [42]. Transvaginal NOTES Retroperitoneoscopy on clinical experience was first described by Zorrón and cols to directly access the left kidney by a vaginal-retroperitoneal tunnel, using a flexible colonoscope with endoscopic insufflation of CO_2 [48].

Fig.4. NOTES Transvaginal Nephrectomy (courtesy Branco and cols, Curitiba, Brazil)

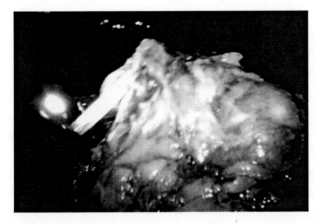

3. Results of NOTES Clinical Experience

IMTN International Multicenter Study

The recent international multicenter IMTN (International Multicenter Trial on Clinical NOTES) study started with a prospective registration began on July of 2007 [15], of the Brazilian NOTES Research Group gradually accepting others participating centers, as a need to evaluate the postoperative results of casuistry of several NOTES procedures, besides register technical improvements.

35

The inclusion of the centers was subject to the approval for owning approval by the Ethics Committee in Research or equivalent, experimental laboratory with adequate resources, flexible endoscopic experience and an available multidisciplinary team. The preliminary results reported will be followed for a minimum period of six years, and the partial results will be published every two years.

OPERATIVE TIME

Before appropriate platforms for NOTES become available, operative time will remain longer than if the standard laparoscopic technique will be used. Despite the lack of appropriate technology for surgery by natural orifice, "Totally NOTES" (T-Notes) surgery was first described in the literature by Sousa and cols[26], using a technique of the insertion of two vaginal endoscopes, and by Gumbs and cols[27] and Davila and cols[28.] using rigid transvaginal instrumentation.

Curiously, if T-NOTES is used, without laparoscopic assistance, the operative time is significantly greater than with any kind of assistance through laparoscopic via for retraction or visualization. The desired triangulation is not possible using the endoscope, and the "in line" dissection techniques, similar to digestive endoscopy, was often described by the centers. The difficulties in applying traction, the lack of multiplanar instrumentation and limited size of the working channels of the endoscope are others obstacles.

In preliminary results of the IMTN study, transgastric NOTES cholecystectomy and transvaginal NOTES had an average of 96.1min and 110.9min respectively, and transgastric and transvaginal NOTES appendicectomy, respectively 135.5min and 60.5min[15]. The time decreased significantly in the case of the introduction of one or more trocars for retraction or dissection, clearly showing that the technical and instrumental development is necessary for future procedures.

Orientation and visualization were not important questions, since all multidisciplinary groups had previous techniques tested in the set of experimental studies or training in animals. The hybrid surgery with laparoscopic assistance was necessary in many cases of more advanced procedures, and in all cases of transgastric surgery.

The initial access by gastrotomy using the endoscope was followed by the safe laparoscopic visualization and allowed low incidence of puncture accidents. The closure of the gastrotomy was always performed by laparoscopic suturing, and sometimes with innovative methods, using only two trocars (3 mm to an optics and 5 mm to an external knotted suture), ensuring the safe recovery, without compromising the cosmetic, until that other effective and safe methods are universally approved. Although one episode of postoperative peritonitis occurred after TG surgery, it was not related to inadequate closure or fistula, and no TV case became infected.

POSTOPERATIVE ANALGESIA

The use of analgesics is an important area of research for NOTES in clinical studies, since better results may be indicate than therapy through laparoscopic via and standard open. Non-randomized studies comparing with laparoscopic cholecystectomy at scientific meetings have shown results of less pain and less need for postoperative analgesics than by the laparoscopic via[49].

The absorption of CO_2 measured by final-tidal CO_2 may also represent a trend and differences in other studies. Other published reports suggest a lower intra-abdominal pressure required for NOTES compared with laparoscopy. In some cases, the procedures were possible using 5 to 6 mmHg of CO_2, possibly due to less need for exposition and insufflation [46]. Although these results could also contribute to less need for analgesia in surgery by natural orifices, these suggestions have not been confirmed.

OPERATIVE COMPLICATIONS

In total, 59 complications were registered in 617 cases in human casuistry in the literature (9.6%). In the IMTN study, the rate of intraoperative complications was 5.48% and the postoperative rate of 2.87%.

Transvaginal NOTES procedures had fewer complications Grade I-II and Grade III-IV than the transgastric NOTES surgery. There were no deaths in the studies published, however there was at least one patient with the possibility of fatal postoperative evolution due to mediastinitis and esophageal perforation.

Grade III-IV complications were observed in 10 patients (2.76%), represented by intra-operative hemorrhage, intestinal damage (recognized and treated intraoperatively), biliary fistula and injury of the esophagus.

Postoperative peritonitis by S. faecalis occurred after one case of transgastric cholecystectomy, although no leakage of the site of the gastric closure. Biliary fistula occurred in two patients after transvaginal surgery, but did not occur due to failure of endoscopic clips, which were not used in cases.

The biliary escape was caused due to the inefficient laparoscopic closure of cystic duct with clips or sutures. There was no iatrogenic injury of the biliary via. Infection is a concern since the beginning of the experimental concept of surgery by natural orifices[50], but has rarely been reported in human literature.

Established methods for gastric and vaginal disinfection, sterilization of instruments and high-level disinfection of flexible endoscopes proved to be satisfactory in this beginning of casuistry in preventing surgical infection.

In the largest series of laparoscopic cholecystectomy, iatrogenic biliary lesions are found in 0.2 to 3% of the literature, but most of the centers individually reported an average rate of 0.3%[51-55]. Major complications are reported in 2-4% and minor complications in 5-7% for laparoscopic cholecystectomy. The mortality rate for laparoscopic cholecystectomy is estimated at less than 0.1%[56].

A longer learning curve for transgastric surgery is expected. Due to lack of adequate instruments to perform dissection and retraction, the need for retroflexion, the need for competence in flexible endoscopy, and the small dimensions of the esophageal lumen certainly contribute to increased operative times and complications than transvaginal NOTES. The use of gastroesophageal overtubes can prevent esophageal injury, as well as avoiding the technical difficulties for the recovery of the specimen, but the instruments and platforms that will be proposed by the industry will have more restrictions on the size and shape than the vaginal and colonic access.

GENERAL RECOMMENDATIONS

Based on the results of published studies, suggestion of general recommendations of future clinical trials are:

Taxonomy for NOTES Procedures. "Totally NOTES" (T-Notes) are procedures performed through any natural orifices without percutaneous assistance. Hybrid NOTES implies the use of laparoscopy for retraction and visualization, but with significant dissection performed through natural orifices.

NOTES-assisted Laparoscopy are operations performed laparoscopically with the contribution of low natural orifice instrumentation (retraction or visualization) as culdolaparoscopy. NOSE *(Natural Orifice Specimen Extraction)* refers to the extraction of specimen by natural orifice as previously published[57]. The differentiation between NOTES performed by flexible endoscopy (FLEX-NOTES) and those performed by rigid instruments (RIG-NOTES) seems to be an important data recording, because flexible instruments are not universally accepted as intra-abdominal surgical arsenal, and due to difficulties in reliable sterilization.

Human Studies. Clinical trials for transgastric, transvaginal transcolonic and approaches must be approved by the local Committee of Ethics in Research, because they are still considered procedures in the context of clinical evaluation, being preferably performed by a multidisciplinary team with qualified endoscopist, and extensive previous experience in animal model. The transesophageal and transurethral access are still inadequate for clinical studies, because of lack of experimental data and technical development for its safe use in trials. Transvaginal NOTES surgery, however, already has major series by several international centers, no longer considered experimental.

Single Access Surgery. Umbilical laparoscopic surgery, or LESS (Laparoendoscopic Single Site Surgery), SAS (Single Access Surgery), SPA (Single Port Access) is not considered surgery by natural orifice, since the navel is a natural scar, not an orifice, and it produces somatic pain to the incision instead of visceral pain found in NOTES. In relation to this concept in evolution, potential advantages in NOTES for prevention of complications related to the incision and also decreased postoperative somatic pain are absent in surgery by single umbilical access.

Feasibility and Safety. Transgastric and transvaginal basic procedures are feasible with the available instruments, and possibly longer operative time than the laparoscopy until emerge new endoscopic technologies. The transvaginal surgery is feasible and safe for simple indications, although transgastric surgery needs the evolution of technology to broader clinical application. The Gastrotomy access still needs closure by laparoscopic suture and preoperative gastric lavage with antiseptic for patient safety. The use of overtubes to perform transgastric NOTES can minimize esophageal complications. Transcolonic access can be safely performed for surgery of the colon with the puncture site to perform the colonic anastomosis, but transcolonic approach to other organs is still under evaluation. Determining the safety of each procedure can only be ensured after the next steps of multicenter and randomized studies with larger numbers of patients by procedure and follow-up time longer.

Learning Curve. Transgastric NOTES initially presented a longer learning curve and higher complication rate than vaginal surgery, due to the difficulty of navigation, spatial orientation, the small size of the light of the organ (esophagus) allowed to work maneuvers, and the need for a secure entry and closure of gastric wall. The flexible surgery has a learning curve harder than rigid NOTES. These barriers will possibly delay the acceptance and development of clinical transgastric surgery, as the access has a limitation of instruments and sizes of specimen extraction.

Sterilization and Preparation. Although the occurrence of infectious complications is relatively low in all studies, efforts must be directed to the production of flexible endoscope, capable of being sterilized in available methods and improvement of cost-effectiveness of methods. Currently, some groups still accept a high-level disinfection, while others have sterilized endoscopes. Intraoperative gastric lavage with chlorhexidine and traditional vaginal disinfection, together with antibiotic prophylaxis can reduce infection.

Contraindications. The procedures are well selected and performed by a specialized team in flexible endoscopy to avoid long operative times and misorientation, anterior pelvic and abdominal surgery, as well as adherences there are more contraindications. Advanced and emergency procedures must be avoided in the initial phase of technological development. For transvaginal access, patients with previous hysterectomy, vaginal infection, pregnancy, endometriosis and naive patients are contraindicated for the procedure. NOTES oncologic procedures has no foundation in literature, but possibly will follow the same pattern of acceptance as laparoscopy. Possibilities of tumor implantation in NOTES is a matter for future research.

Indications. So far, none of the procedures performed in studies around the world proved to be superior in relation to laparoscopic surgery. Suggested advantages, such as less intra-abdominal pressure, less pain demonstrated by one percentage of patients with non-use of postoperative analgesia and less incisional complications can also be considered for future research.

SUMMARY OF RESULTS OF CLINICAL APPLICATIONS

NOTES seems to be evolving as a viable, safe and reasonable option for abdominal surgery, with the potential to completely avoid the complications related to incisions. However, caution is necessary, as complications experienced during the early days of laparoscopic surgery must not be repeated.

Despite the long operative time, these preliminary results of the literature demonstrated acceptable rates of complications in all international centers, with low hospital stay, less postoperative pain, and with good cosmetic results, especially for transvaginal surgery. Future prospective clinical studies comparing NOTES with laparoscopy may be necessary, to evaluate if the new technologies are effective and reproducible [58]. More important than this and perhaps crucial to indicate a long life for transluminal surgery, will return to be the skill of surgeons and endoscopists to replace complex surgical procedures for easier endoscopic procedures, as well as the identification of new therapeutic targets[59].

Therefore, it is expected that more clinical studies can reproduce these results, and adding substantial evolution in patient care.

REFERENCES

1. Rao GV, Reddy DN, Banerjee R. NOTES: Human Experience. Gastrintest Endoscopy Clin N Am 2008; 18: 361-370.

2. Kalloo AN, Singh VK, Jagannath BS, Niiyama H, Hill SL, Vaughn CA, Magee CA, Kantsevoy SV. Flexible transgastric peritoneoscopy: a novel approach to diagnostic and therapeutic interventions in the peritoneal cavity. Gastrointest Endosc 2004; 60(1): 287-292.

3. Delvaux G, Devroey P, De Waele B, et al. Transvaginal removal of gallbladders with large stones after laparoscopic cholecystectomy. Surg Laparosc Endosc 1993 3(4): 307-309.

4. Breda G, Silvestre P, Giunta A, et al. Laparoscopic nephrectomy with vaginal delivery of the intact kidney. Eur Urol 1993; 24(1):116-117.

5. Zornig C, Emmerman A, von Waldenfels HA, et al. Colpotomy for specimen removal in laparoscopic surgery. Chirurg 1994; 65(10): 883-885.

6. Seifert H, Wehrmann T, Schmit T, et al. Retroperitoneal endoscopic debridement for infected peripancreatic necrosis. Lancet 2000; 19(356): 653-655.

7. Rattner D, Kalloo, A. ASGE/SAGES Working Group on Natural Orifice Translumenal Endoscopic Surgery. Surg Endosc 2006; 20: 329-333.

8. Zorron R, Filgueiras M, Maggioni LC, Pombo L, Carvalho GL, Oliveira AL. NOTES Transvaginal cholecystectomy: Report of the first case. Surg Innov 2007; 14(4): 279-283.

9. Zorron R, Maggioni LC, Pombo L, Oliveira AL, Carvalho GL, Filgueiras M. NOTES Transvaginal cholecystectomy: Preliminary clinical application. Surg Endosc 2008; 22(2): 542-547.

10. Branco Filho AJ, Noda RW, Kondo W, Kawahara N, Rangel M, Branco AW. Initial experience with hybrid transvaginal cholecystectomy. Gastrointest Endosc. 2007; 66(6):1245-1248.

11. Marescaux J, Dallemagne B, Perretta S, Wattiez A, Mutter D, Coumaros D. Report of transluminal cholecystectomy in a human being. Arch Surg 2007; 142: 823-826.

12. Zornig C, Emmerman A, von Waldenfels HA, Mofid H. Laparoscopic cholecystectomy without visible scar: combined transvaginal and transumbilical approach. Endoscopy 2007; 39(10): 913-915.

13. Ramos AC, Murakami A, Galvão Neto M, Galvão MS, Silva AC, Canseco EG, Moyses Y. NOTES Transvaginal video-assisted cholecystectomy: first series. Endoscopy 2008; 40(7):572-575.

14. Bessler M, Stevens PD, Milone L, Parikh M, Fowler D. Transvaginal laparoscopically-assisted endoscopic cholecystectomy: a hybrid approach to natural orifice surgery. Gastrointest Endosc 2007; 66(6): 1243-1245.

15. Zorron R, Palanivelu C, Galvão Neto MP, Ramos A, Salinas G, Burghardt J, Decarli L, Henrique Sousa L, Forgione A, Pugliese R, Branco AJ, Balashanmugan TS, Boza C, Corcione F, D'Avila Avila F, Arturo Gómez N, Galvão Ribeiro PA, Martins S, Filgueiras M, Gellert K, Wood Branco A, Kondo W, Inacio Sanseverino J, de Sousa JA, Saavedra L, Ramírez E, Campos J, Sivakumar K, Pidigu Seshiyer Rajan, Priyadarshan Anand Jategaonkar, Ranagrajan M, Parthasarathi R, Senthilnathan P, Prasad M, Cuccurullo D, Müller V. International Multicenter Trial on Clinical Natural Orifice Surgery--NOTES IMTN Study: Preliminary Results of 362 Patients.Surg Innov. 2010 Jun;17(2):142-58. PMID: 20504792

16. Decker A, Cherry TH. Culdoscopy- a new method in the diagnosis of pelvic disease- preliminary report. Am J Surg 1944; 64: 40-44.

17. Christian J, Barrier BF, Schust D, et al. Culdoscopy: a foundation for Natural Orifice Surgery- past, present and future. J Am Coll Surg 2008; Set 207 (3): 417-422.

18. Bueno B. Primer caso de apendicectomia por via vaginal. Tokoginec Pract (Madrid) 1949; 8: 152-154.

19. Reiner IJ. Incidental appendectomy at the time of vaginal surgery. Texas Med 1980: 46-50.

20. Tsin DA, Colombero L, Mahmood D, Padouvas J, Manolas P. Operative culdolaparoscopy: a new approach combining operative culdoscopy and minilaparoscopy. J Am Assoc Gynecol Laparosc 2001;8(3):438-441.

21. DeCarli L, Zorron R, Branco A, Lima FC, Tang M, Pioneer SR, Sanseverino JI, Menguer R, Bigolin AV, Gagner M. New hybrid approach for NOTES transvaginal cholecystectomy: Preliminary clinical experience. Surg Innov 2009; 16(20):181-186.

22. Forgione A, Maggioni D, Sansonna F, Ferrari C, Di Lernia S, Citterio D, Magistro C, Frigerio L, Pugliese R. Transvaginal endoscopic cholecystectomy in human beings: preliminary results. J Laparoendosc Adv Surg Tech A. 2008; 18(3):345-351.

23. Noguera J, Dolz C, Cuadrado A, Olea J, Vilella A, Morales R. Hybrid transvaginal cholecystectomy, NOTES, and minilaparoscopy: analysis of a prospective clinical series. Surg Endosc 2009; 23: 876-881.

24. Palanivelu C, Rajan PS, Rangarajan M, Prasad M, Kalyanakumari V, Parthasarathi R, Senthilnathan P. Transvaginal endoscopic cholecystectomy in humans: preliminary report of a case series. Am J Gastroenterol. 2009;104(4):843-847.

25. Horgan S, Cullen JP, Talamini MA, Mintz Y, Ferreres A, Jacobsen GR, Sandler B, Bosia J, Savides T, Easter DW, Savu MK, Ramamoorthy SL, Whitcomb E, Agarwal S, Lukacz E, Dominguez G, Ferraina P. Natural orifice surgery: initial clinical experience. Surg Endosc 2009; 23(7): 1512-1518.

26. Sousa LH, Sousa JAG, Sousa MM, Sousa VM, APM Sousa , Zorrón R.TOTALLY NOTE.S (T-NOTES) Transvaginal Cholecystectomy using Two Endoscopes: Preliminary report. Surg Endosc 2009; *epub ahead of print.* PMID: 19343424 [PubMed - as supplied by publisher]

27. Gumbs AA, Fowler D, Milone L, Evanko JC, Ude AO, Stevens P, Bessler M. Transvaginal natural endoscopic surgery cholecystectomy: early evolution of the technique. Ann Surg 2009; 249 (6): 908-912.

28. Davila F, Tsin DA, Dominguez G, Davila U, Jesús R, Gomez de Arteche A. Transvaginal cholecystectomy without abdominal ports. JSLS. 2009;13(2):213-216.

29. Palanivelu C, Rajan PS, Rangarajan M, Parthasarathi R, Senthilnathan P, Prasad M. Transvaginal endoscopic appendectomy in humans: a unique approach to NOTES-world's first report. Surg Endosc 2008; 22(5):1343-1347.

30. Bernhardt J, Gerber B, Schober HJ, Kähler G, Ludwig K. NOTES- case report of a unidirectional flexible appendectomy. Int J Colorectal Dis 2008; 23:547-550.

31. Lacy AM, Delgado S, Rojas OA, Almenara R, Blasi A, Llach J. MA-NOS radical sigmoidectomy: report of a transvaginal resection in the human. Surg Endosc 2008; 22(7): 1717-1723.

32. Burghardt J, Federlein M, Müller V, Benhidjeb T, Elling D, Gellert K. Minimal invasive transvaginal right hemicolectomy: report of the first complex NOS (natural orifice surgery) bowels operation using a hybrid approach. Zentralbl Chir. 2008 Dec;133(6):574-6.

33. Ramos AC, Zundel N, Neto MG, Maalouf M. Human hybrid NOTES transvaginal sleeve gastrectomy: initial experience. Surg Obes Relat Dis. 2008;4(5):660-663.

34. Fischer LJ, Jacobsen G, Wong B, Thompson K, Bosia J, Talamini M, Horgan S. NOTES laparoscopic-assisted transvaginal sleeve gastrectomy in humans--description of preliminary experience in the United States. Surg Obes Relat Dis. 2009; 5(5):633-636.

35. Zorron R. Techniques of transvaginal access for NOTES. Tech Gastrointest Endosc 2009; 11: 75-83.

36. Salinas G, Saavedra L, Aqurto H, Quispe R, Ramirez E, Grande J, Tamayo J, Sánchez V, Málaga D, Marks JM. Early experience in human transgastric and transvaginal endoscopic cholecystectomy. Surg Endosc 2009 Dec 8. [Epub ahead of print] PMID: 19997754 [PubMed - as supplied by publisher]

37. Marks JM, Ponsky JL, Pearl JP, McGee MF. PEG rescue: a practical NOTES technique. Surg Endosc. 2007; 21(5): 816-819.

38. Hazey JW, Narula VK, Renton DB, Reavis KM, Paul CM, Hinshaw KE, Muscarella P, Ellison EC, Melvin WS. Natural orifice transgastric endoscopic peritoneoscopy in humans: initial clinical trial. Surg Endosc 2008; 22: 16-20.

39. Dallemagne B, Perretta S, Allemann P, Asakuma M, Marescaux J. Transgastric hybrid cholecystectomy. Br J Surg 2009; 96: 1162–1166.

40. Auyang ED, Hungness ES, Vaziri K, Martin JA, Soper NJ. Human NOTES cholecystectomy: transgastric hybrid technique. J Gastrointest Surg. 2009; 13(6): 1149-1150.

41. DDW 2009 Annual Meeting- May 30-June 4 2009, Chicago, IL.

42. Gettman MT, Blute ML. Transvesical peritoneoscopy: initial clinical evaluation of the bladder as a portal for natural orifice translumenal endoscopic surgery. Mayo Clin Proc. 2007 Jul;82(7):843-5.

43. Buess G, Kipfmüller K, Ibald R, Heintz A, Hack D, Brausntein S, Gabbert H. Junginger T. Clinical results of transanal endoscopic microsurgery. Surg Endosc 1988; 2 : 245-250.

44. Zorron R. Natural Orifice Surgery applied to colorectal diseases. World J Gastrointest Surg 2010; 27;2 (2): 35-38.

45. Zorron R, Coelho D, Flach L, Lemos FB, Moreira MS, Oliveira PS, Barbosa AM. Cirurgia por orificios naturais transcolônica: Acesso NOTES Prei-retal (PNA) para excisão mesorretal total. Rev Bras Coloproct 2010; 30 (1): 14-22.

46. Zorron R, Soldan M, Filgueiras M, Maggioni LC, Pombo L, Oliveira AL. NOTES Transvaginal for cancer diagnostic staging: Preliminary clinical application. Surg Innov 2008 15(3):161-165.

47. Branco AW, Branco Filho AJ, Condo W, Noda RW, Kawahara N, Camargo AA, Stunitz LC, Valente J, Rangel M. Hybrid transvaginal nephrectomy. Eur Urol. 2008 53(6):1290-4.

48. Zorron R, Goncalves L, Leal D, Kanaan E, Cabral I, Saraiva P. Transvaginal hybrid natural orifice transluminal endoscopic surgery retroperitoneoscopy- the first human case report. J Endourol. 2009 Dec 29. [Epub ahead of print]PMID: 20039826 [PubMed - as supplied by publisher]

49. Zorron R. Human work to date, an international perspective [oral presentation]. In: Update on NOTES. The SAGES Annual Meeting, April 10, 2008.

50. Kantsevoy SV. Infection Prevention in NOTES. Gastrintest Endoscopy Clin N Am 2008; 18: 291-296.

51. Larson G, Vitale G, Casey J, et al. Multipractice analysis of of laparoscopic cholecystectomies in 1,093 patients. Am J Surg 1992; 163: 221-226.

52. Rossi R, Shirmer W, Braasch J, et al. Laparoscopic bile duct injuries: risk factors, recognition and repair. Arch Surg 1992; 127: 596-601.

53. MacMahon AJ, Fullarton G, Baxter JN, Dwyer PJ. Bile duct injury and bile leakage in laparoscopic cholecystectomy. Br J Surg 1995; 82: 307-313.

54. Quinn S, Sangster W, Standale B, et al. Biliary complications related to laparoscopic cholecystectomies: radiologic diagnosis and management. Surg Laparosc Endosc 1992; 2: 279-286.

55. Strasberg SM, Hertl M, Soper NJ, et al. An analysis of the problem of biliary injury during laparoscopic cholecystectomy. J Am Coll Surg 1995; 180: 101-125.

56. Steiner CA, Bass EB, Talamini MA, et al. Surgical rates and operative mortality for open and laparoscopic cholecystectomy in Maryland. N Engl J Med 1994; 330: 403-408.

57. Palanivelu C, Rangarajan M, Jategaonkar PA, Anand NV. An innovative technique for colorectal specimen retrieval: a new era of "natural orifice

specimen extraction" (N.O.S.E). Dis Colon Rectum. 2008; 51(7):1120-1124.

58. Sodergreen MH, Clark J, Athanasiou T, et al. Natural orifice translumenal endoscopic rurgery: critical appraisal of applications in clinical practice. Surg Endosc 2009; 23(4): 680-687.

59. Pasricha PJ, Krummel TM. NOTES and other emerging trends in gastrointestinal endoscopy and surgery: The change that we need and the change that is real. Am J Gastroenterol 2009; 104: 2384-2386.

NOTES HYBRID SURGERY

LUIZ ALBERTO DE CARLI

MARCOS TANG

FERNANDO CREBS CIRNE LIMA

ANDRÉ VICENTE BIGOLIN

"Fear not for the future, Weep not for the past."

Percy Bysshe Shelley, 1792–1822

INTRODUCTION

Per se surgery and surgeons are looking for innovation and improvement in their techniques. With the influence of technological evolution it became possible, in the late '80s, the idealization of a new surgical technique - the videolaparoscopic (VLP) [1]. In conjunction with the emergence of promising better results came to light the urgent need for adaptation and learning of the abdominal surgeons. As idealized by their patients, "laser surgery" began a chain of animal experiments and studies of initial application with the objective of reducing the learning curve and overcome the limitations still imposed by the inexperienced use of the laparoscope. The loss of depth perception, tactile sensation and the restriction of the instrumental movement were overcome and the advantages of the VLP are now appreciated and considered standard in a range of procedures [2,3].

When we imagined that a new surgical paradigm could not come up with the same impact, Kalloo and Kantsevoy (2000) presented their experience with transgastric gastrojejunostomy in animal model [3]. Four years later, this same author has planted a landmark in endoscopic surgery through natural orifices (NOTES) with the initial publication of transgastric peritoneoscope [4]. The distrust and chaos in the scientific race during this period were not the only similarities with the emergence of VLP. The obstacles to be overcome were not significantly different.

Thus emerged the NOSCAR (Natural Orifice Consortium of Assessment and Research Committee), a group of members formed by surgeons and endoscopists that through these three focuses are focused on evolution of NOTES: 1. research; 2. education; 3. creation and maintenance of a record.

Close to the creation of this group, it was produced the so-called White Paper, the result of the work of two societies and it serves as a parameter for the development of NOTES [5,6].

The theoretical advantages of NOTES (Table 1) are extremely promising; but, it is necessary to break some barriers for their clinical practice (Table 2). The lack of practice with the access by natural orifices and the restricted availability of appropriate flexible materials are considered the most important factors among the causes of difficulty in the application of NOTES.

Table 1. Theoretical Advantages of NOTES [5,6]

→ Decrease in infections of the abdominal wall
→ Less formation of adherences
→ Less adynamic ileus
→ Faster recovery
→ Less pain
→ Absence of abdominal incisional hernias
→ Surgery with perfect cosmetic appearance
→ Less invasive

Table 2. Potential barriers for the clinical practice of NOTES 5,6
→ Access to the peritoneal cavity
→ Gastric Closure (intestinal)
→ Prevention of infections
→ Development of suturing devices
→ Spatial orientation
→ Development of platforms for performing the procedures
→ Control of intraperitoneal hemorrhage
→ Management of iatrogenic intraperitoneal complications
→ Inconvenient physiological events
→ Compressive syndromes
→ Training

Emerges then the need to perform an endoscopic surgery, however, aided by appropriate instruments, with the direct analysis of the procedure, the expansion of two-dimensional view, better triangulation and precision of each movement and therefore less learning curve. This would be the necessary bridge in the transition between laboratory experiments and the actual clinical application of NOTES. Front of this scenario prevailed the creativity of the surgeon and so it was created a hybrid technique, that combines the use of an endoscope by a natural orifice and the help of videolaparoscopic instrumental[7].

PROCEDURE OF CHOICE AND VIA OF ACCESS

In animal models a huge variety of procedures have been performed, including the creation of anastomosis, appendectomy, tubal ligation, lymphadenectomy and splenectomy [2,8-11]. In a systematic literature review, until the year 2007, five studies reported the performance of cholecystectomy in animals, with a success rate ranging between 33% and 100% [10,12-16]. In humans, another similarity in relation to the emergence of VLP is found when we refer to the procedure with the widest diffusion in NOTES, cholecystectomy. The custom of the surgeon with this procedure and also the easy access to the surgical site are factors that stimulate this predilection. Other procedures have been performed in humans such as the nephrectomy described by Branco et al. [17]

However, it is not enough randomly choose the procedure to be performed and the access via to the abdominal cavity. Despite the use of high-level endoscopic techniques, such as the retroflexion and rotation, many accesses make it difficult to visualize structures and performing procedures. The performance of maneuvers with the equipment in the upper abdominal quadrants can bring some difficulties when transgastric access is used. The need for lateralization and inversion of image limit the movements and distort the spatial orientation. However when the portal of access is the colon these difficulties seem to intensify [18].

The difficulty of pulling and manipulating organs during NOTES is also affected by local access as well as the proximity of the body with this site [19]. The peculiarity of the cholecystectomy, by requiring the retraction of the hepatic lobe such as the exposition of the Trine of Callot, requires a disposition of the endoscope in the cavity that allows the greatest possible mobility in the maneuvers.

The choice of the access orifice to the peritoneal cavity still faces the limitation imposed by endoscopic materials used for its synthesis. Although the initial idealization of NOTES being through a transgastric approach, about the closure of this, several techniques have been demonstrated, but none seems to provide adequate security. Among them have been used clips, rivets, endoscopic sutures and even endoloops [14, 20-22].

Swanstrom et al. demonstrated a complete closure rate of 93% of gastrostomy, however, only 17% of the closures have demonstrated efficacy when tested after surgery [16]. Some authors, after using the gastric via found formation of abscess and positive culture of bacteria in the peritoneal cavity due to bad closure of the orifice[19, 22]. In the study of Sumiyama et al 2 animals needed to be sacrificed due to peritonitis caused by gastric contents[16].

The closure of a natural orifice by endoscopy is considered a highly complex procedure. Pham et al reported that the success rate of colostomy closure in animals is directly related to the experience of the endoscopist responsible for the procedure[24]. The use of videolaparoscopic instrumentals may be the initial solution to the closure of the natural orifices untill the adequate materials will be developed and prove their effectiveness.

Large part of the mortality reported in studies in an experimental model is referred to the failure of the closure of the viscerotomy. These results suggest a direct relationship between bad closure of the entrance orifice and an unfavorable prognosis. However, some studies report favorable outcomes without the closure, which could only be explained by the peculiarities of the physiology of the animal used[12].

Preliminary studies in humans have used the more plausible and reasonable access to clinical application of NOTES, the transvaginal access[25-27]. With the results presented by these authors and also with the current technology so far, it is believed that a hybrid technique to perform cholecystectomy that combines vision, but also the use of endoscopic forceps and the aid of VLP, must be the procedure considered as the choice for transition and adjustment to NOTES.

The access by vaginal via allows the closure of the orifice by direct visualization and thus break many barriers related to the inability of instrumentals of synthesis. This access, what was already described and extensively explored by gynecologists, is characterized by a lower risk of bacterial contamination, good distensibility for the passage of high-caliber materials and platforms, as well as good ergonomic conditions of operability of to the surgeon, factors reported by Stark and Benhidjeb[28]. Therefore the surgical technique described below is directed to perform transvaginal cholecystectomy in humans, and it was developed by the authors for primary application of NOTES in 20 cases.

SURGICAL TECHNIQUE

It is describe two forms of hybrid NOTES. The surgery can be performed using the laparoscopic view, through the optics introduced by trocar in the abdominal wall and thus use the flexible instruments for endoscopic procedures. The second option, referred to as the preferred by the authors, uses the endoscopic instrumentals and the VLP, already consecrated to perform surgery[7].

Patients must be submitted to general anesthesia and positioned in the Lloyd-Davies position. As antibioticprophilaxy is used a single bolus of 2.0g of Cefazolin and 400mg of Metronidazole. The antissepia is performed covering the entire abdomen, perineal area and vagina. The pneumoperitoneum is initiated by puncture with Verres Needle and intra-abdominal pressure is maintained at 13mmHg. In the last cases, cavity insufflation was performed directly by the vaginal portal without the need of umbilical puncture. The surgeon must be positioned between the patient's legs, while his assistants are placed one on each side (Fig. 1).

After established the pneumoperitoneum it is performed posterior colpotomy with the help of gynecological valves and under direct vision. After

57

performed the colpotomy a dual channel endoscope, properly sterilized, must be introduced into the abdominal cavity. The entrance of the endoscope can be facilitated by performing the Trendelenburg position. Under endoscopic view must be performed the placement of two umbilical portals of 3 mm and another portal of 10 mm placed by vaginal via and parallel to the endoscope (Fig. 2). This trocar was especially developed by the authors in conjunction with the engineering department of the Holy House of Porto Alegre, and increased its length to 30 cm, which allows the entrance and exit of instrumentals with minimized risk of intestinal handles injury (Fig.3).

The dissection of the Trine of Callot must be performed by the umbilical forceps of 3mm with the aid of endoscopic instrumentals such as graspers, hot-biopsy and others flexible instruments. The clip placement of the cystic duct and of the cystic artery are performed by laparoscopic clips by passing a long laparoscopic clipper (42cm, 10mm) by vaginal portal. The entrance of the forceps cavity was observed by retroflexion of the endoscopic device and facilitated by the exchange of decubitus to Trendelenburg.

After sectioned the duct and artery, the gall is detached from the gallbladder bed with the use of laparoscopic hook (3 mm) and endoscopic hook (2 mm). After the review of hemostasis the surgical piece is removed by the vaginal orifice without the use of protective bag. The complacency of the vaginal access allows the removal of the gallbladder even with stones of large diameters without expanding the incision. The closure of colpotomy is performed by suture with under direct vision with absorbable thread.

Antibiotic therapy is not routinely used postoperatively. The need for hospitalization varies according to research protocol, which hospital discharge recommended in the first 48 hours.

Figure 1. Position of the surgical team.

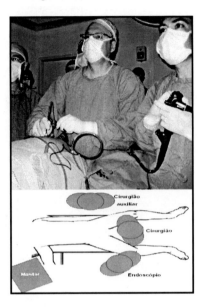

Figure 2. Abdominal portals with 3 mm inserted in the navel scar combined with the transvaginal access for the endoscopic device. Trendelenburg position during the procedure.

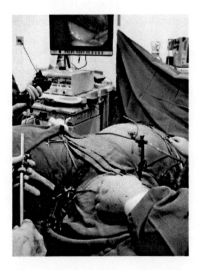

Figure 3: Trocar designed (below) to perform transvaginal hybrid NOTES compared to traditional laparoscopic trocar 10mm (above)

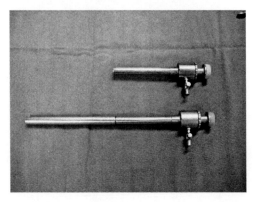

RESULTS AND MAIN FACTOR

The authors mention that the technique described provided the performance of all procedures with a high degree of security. These results support the initial expectations of less pain, quick recovery, decreased surgical time proportional to the learning curve and good acceptance by the patients.

Some factors worth mentioning in this chapter, since, about these, just a little bit is intended in the publications of initial experiments.

Animal Training: The recommendations of NOSCAR recommend the conduction of animal experiments before clinical application of NOTES. No doubt this staff must be followed very strictly. During the phase of experiment the authors could report the low effectiveness of endoscopic clips in the approach of cystic duct and cystic artery. These data have made it to be possible use in human cases a long laparoscopic clipper through vaginal access. This conduct provided greater security and familiarity in the approach of these structures. Other techniques can be used until the appropriate materials to be developed, such as polypropylene endoloops 2.0 used by Zorron et al. [25] The training provides surgeons' familiarity with endoscopic equipment and as the main fact accentuates the real conditions and limitations of the technique.

Spatial Orientation and Image: As in the VLP, perform a surgery in three dimensions through a two-dimensional view is a condition to be offset by surgical skill. The flexibility of the endoscope allows creating a sense of depth to provide images from different angles and can therefore be recreated in the imagination of surgeons. The endoscopic image is referred as high quality, about the visualization and discrimination of the structures. The potential for self-cleaning of the lenses of the device allows them need not to be removed from the cavity until the end of the procedure or extraction of the specimen.

Some maneuvers may facilitate the orientation in the peritoneal cavity. In an example, when entering the endoscope through the posterior colpotomy, Trendelenburg positioning can be helpful; whereas the inverse position should be adopted aiding in the removal of the intestinal handles that stands in the access to the superior abdomen. The retroversion of the endoscope allows visualization of the passage of laparoscopic instrumentals by natural orifice, as well as we can supervise the insertion of abdominal portals. The optics approach to the surgical site and changes in its angulation allows a lower degree of pressure in the pneumoperitoneum than required by the VLP.

Retraction and Exhibition: The VLP, has already demonstrated its advantages about the exposure of the surgical site when compared to open surgery, where the more exposure is required more the incision is enlarged. If we take into account the ability to increase the image by the laparoscope, the delicacy of the movement and the aid of pneumoperitoneum we understand this difference. These benefits are automatically transferred to the NOTES.

But in this, the portal of instrumental entry is the same for removal, dissection and synthesis. Therefore the triangulation of the instrumentals it is impossible and it is complicated a simultaneous work . At this point the hybrid technique break another barrier by allowing, through the aid of hard VLP instrumentals, endoscopic platform to be used in a specific way - sometimes for dissection, sometimes for traction and simultaneously for visualization. This will continue as an option until that an endoscopic platform with flexible and capable instrumentals of triangulation to be developed.

Algesic and immunological effects: The use of a natural orifice aims to obtain a minimally invasive procedure and thus reducing tissue trauma and stimuli to inflammatory factors and pain receptors. Although considered subjective the measurement of postoperative pain can be a parameter directly related to the intensity of tissue damage. Data regarding pain in patients operated by NOTES demonstrate effectiveness of the technique on this parameter. These can be considered susceptible to bias due to be reported with euphoria by applying this new approach. In this way in animal model, studies have tried to prove through analysis of immunological factors what is the standard of inflammatory changes caused by NOTES.

The studies of McGee et al and Bingen et al have hypothesized that this approach can cause a greater insult to the immune system by bacterial contamination associated with site access [29,30]. Nevertheless their results are consistent only in stating that only in NOTES does not cause an overstimulation of the initial inflammatory phase. Being that, this is associated with the possible adverse effects such as severe bacterial growth, multiple organ failure, systemic inflammatory response syndrome and increased mortality. It is worth remembering that these experiments have inherent limitations to the experimental model, but also compared the techniques using only peritoneoscopy, which discourages the endoscopic technique that requires less or no auxiliar portal in the execution of other procedures.

So, it is necessary that human studies to be realized and that especially the role of late postoperative immunosuppression to be established and therefore enables the measurement of the effects of NOTES as deleterious or not to the immune system . The approach with the hybrid technique can help to reduce peritoneal contamination for ensuring the effectiveness in the closure of the viscerotomy.

NEXT STEPS

The next step to be tracked, are quite promising for hybrid NOTES; but the scientific foundation must prevail. After the report of the first case of hybrid NOTES in morbidly obese patient has opened a new field for this technique [31]. The flexible materials used in this case have provided an effective approach of the gallbladder and thus presented to the surgical community as a new ally in overcoming the limitations imposed by the particularities of the obese patient.

After this first step, Ramos et al reported the first cases of Sleeve gastrectomy by hybrid NOTES [32]. In four cases, these authors reported no complications in the use of this technique. There are still limitations when we talk about the the evolution of this procedure to be performed by pure NOTES. These barriers are mainly related to instrumental limitation. With the development of a flexible staple the number of abdominal portals can be significantly reduced and progressively directed to a pure endoscopic technique.

To maintain exponential curve of evolution it is necessary that studies are well delineated, conducted and grounded in scientific principles already established [33]. Poorly conducted studies can become harmful for a certain field when they start to provide impression of overoptimism. With this, they can harm the baseline information and take credit of new studies. Ethical approval it is imperative recommendation of NOSCAR and must be obtained in all cases. Both experimental procedures and in the cases concerned it is worthy questioning how much risk or discomfort is acceptable in the scientific pro.

The informed consent must be obtained from all patients and needs to contain information about the potential risks and optional treatment techniques . Before any mobilization to begin working with NOTES it is crucial to organize a working group [1,3,5,6]. Must be included representatives from areas of veterinary medicine, nursing, endoscopy, gynecology (according to surgical access) and surgery. Only with this multidisciplinary team becomes possible to execute a proper study, allowing from the animal training to the analgesic control , implementation of protocols and evaluation of patient's general clinical conditions. In open surgery the main surgeon coordinates the center of operation and manipulates his assistant according to the necessity of access to the surgical site.

The VLP requires the coordinated action of two assistants for a precise approach. In the NOTES the dependence is even greater, because we must consider that the endoscope manipulated by one will direct the action of clamps operated by another professional. The surgical field is smaller and the dispute of space must be harmonious. Greater care must be observed when using more than one hole as in the hybrid technique, because using rigid instruments simultaneously together with the flexible instruments can be a challenge.

FINAL CONSIDERATIONS

The application of a new technique must not only obey the scientific commitment and innovative impetus of the surgeons, but especially must consider the opinion of those who will be treated by it. Swanstrom et al demonstrated that when patients were asked about the choice between the VLP and NOTES to perform their cholecystectomy, they valued more the risk of complications, time to recovery and postoperative pain than cosmetic aspects, cost, length of hospital stay and type of anesthesia [34].

The most interested professionals place in the background the so exalted concept of surgery without scars. Having in mind the NOTES as a surgery without incisions it is a great illusion. The abdominal scars are replaced by a viscerotomy. During the evolution of flexible endoscopy and VLP their ways collided and resulted in the emergence of NOTES. Nevertheless this product of the innovation techniques bumped into physiological inexperience and lack of support materials, diverting its course and going back to something more palpable, the hybridization of the technique [35].

VLP and NOTES must not be considered enemies or competitors techniques. It is up to surgeons to rationalize and use the synergy of these different approaches aiming at the commitment to the final outcome of the procedure and not the surgical technique to be employed.

The use of access through the stomach, colon and bladder still requires technological subsidies not very effective currently. The first cases of endoscopic transgastric peritoneoscope have been reported without major complications, but the closure of the vicetoromy has not been adequately evaluated [197]. The transvaginal via includes the necessary features, being, that, the probable procedure of choice in the transition to application of the pure NOTES.

Even if improbable, if the evolution of the NOTES was frozen, its legacy to modern surgery already pay all commitment and effort credited to it. The trend of the use of flexible materials increased so much the VLP when it has enabled the emergence of a new technique for transumbilical surgery by single portal (*Single Port Laparoscopy*). The endoscopic platforms, unchanged since its introduction 50 years ago, today presents in a new generation with greater mobility and channels of instrumentation [7]. Thus, innovation adds to the procedure and not just the means, be it VLP, NOTES, or, better, their combination.

REFERENCES

1. Mintz Y., Talamini M.A., Cullen J. Evolution of Laparoscopic Surgery: Lessons for NOTES. Gastrointest Endoscopy Clin N Am; 18 (2008) 225–234.

2. Jagannath SB, Kantsevoy SV, Vaughn CA, et al. Peroral transgastric endoscopic ligation of fallopian tubes with long-term survival in a porcine model. Gastrointest Endosc 2005; 61(3): 449–53.

3. Hawes R.H. Transition from Laboratory to Clinical Practice in NOTES: Role of NOSCAR. Gastrointest Endoscopy Clin N Am 18 (2008) 333–341.

4. Kalloo A, Singh VK, Jagannath SB, et al. Flexible transgastric peritoneoscopy: a novel approach to diagnostic and therapeutic interventions in the peritoneal cavity. Gastrointest Endosc 2004; 60(1):114–7.

5. Rattner D, Kalloo A. ASGE/SAGES Working Group on Natural Orifice Translumenal Endoscopic Surgery. October 2005. Surg Endosc 2006;20(2):329–33.

6. Kalloo A, Datlner D. ASGE/SAGES Working Group on Natural Orifice Translumenal Endoscopic Surgery. White Paper October 2005. Gastrointest Endosc 2006;63(2):199–203.

7. Pearl J., Marks J.M., Ponsky J.L.. Hybrid Surgery: Combined Laparoscopy and Natural Orifice Surgery. Gastrointest Endoscopy Clin N Am 18 (2008) 325–332.

8. Bergstrom M, Ikeda K, Swain P, et al. Transgastric anastomosis by using flexible endoscopy in a porcine model. Gastrointest Endos. 2006;63:307–312.

9. Sumiyama K, Gostout CJ, Rajan E, et al. Pilot study of the porcine uterine horn as an in vivo appendicitis model for development of endoscopic transgastric appendectomy. Gastrointest Endosc. 2006;64: 808–812.

10. Fritscher-Ravens A, Mosse CA, Ikeda K, et al. Endoscopic transgastric lymphadenectomy by using EUS for selection and guidance. Gastrointest Endosc. 2006;63:302–306.

11. Kantsevoy SV, Hu B, Jagannath SB, et al. Transgastric endoscopic splenectomy—is it possible? Surg Endosc. 2006;20:522–525

12. Della Flora E, Wilson T.G., Martin I.J., O'Rourke N.A., Maddern G.J. A Review of Natural Orifice Translumenal Endoscopic Surgery (NOTES) for Intra-abdominal Surgery. Experimental Models, Techniques, and Applicability to the Clinical Setting. Ann Surg 2008;247: 583–602

13. Swanstrom LL, Kozarek R, Pasricha PJ, et al. Development of a new access device for transgastric surgery. J Gastrointest Surg. 2005;9: 1129–1136.

14. Pai RD, Fong DG, Bundga ME, et al. Transcolonic endoscopic cholecystectomy: a NOTES survival study in a porcine model. Gastrointest Endosc. 2006;64:428–434.

15. Park PO, Bergstrom M, Ikeda K, et al. Experimental studies of transgastric gallbladder surgery: cholecystectomy and cholecystogastric anastomosis. Gastrointest Endosc. 2005;61:601– 606.

16. Sumiyama K, Gostout CJ, Rajan E, et al. Transgastric cholecystectomy: transgastric accessibility to the gallbladder improved with the SEMF method and a novel multibending therapeutic endoscope. Gastrointest Endosc. 2007;65:1028 –1034.

17. Branco AW, Filho AJ, Kondo W, Noda RW, Kawahara N, Camargo AA, Stunitz LC, Valente J, Rangel M. Hybrid Transvaginal Nephrectomy. Eur Urol. 2007 Nov 5

18. Fong DG, Pai RD, Thompson CC. Transcolonic endoscopic abdominal exploration: a NOTES survival study in a porcine model. Gastrointest Endosc. 2007;65:312–318.

19. Hazey JW, Narula VK, Renton DB, et al. Natural-orifice transgastric endoscopic peritoneoscopy in humans: initial clinical trial. Surg Endosc. 2007.

20. Hu B, Chung SC, Sun LC, Kawashima K, Yamamoto T, Cotton PB, Gostout CJ, Hawes RH, Kalloo AN, Kantsevoy SV, Pasricha PJ (2005) Transoral obesity surgery: endoluminal gastroplasty with an endoscopic suture device. Endoscopy 37:411–414

21. Hausmann U, Feussner H, Ahrens P, Heinzl J (2006) Endoluminal endosurgery: rivet application in flexible endoscopy. Gastrointest Endosc 64:101–103

22. M. F. McGee, J. M. Marks, R. P. Onders, A. Chak, J. Jin, C. P. Williams, S. J. Schomisch, J. L. Ponsky. Complete Endoscopic Closure of Gastrotomy After Natural

Orifice Translumenal Endoscopic Surgery Using the NDO Plicator. Surg Endosc (2008) 22:214–220

23. Wagh MS, Merri.eld BF, Thompson CC (2006) Survival studies after endoscopic transgastric oophorectomy and tubectomy in a porcine model. Gastrointest Endosc 63: 473–478

24. Pham BV, Raju GS, Ahmed I, et al. Immediate endoscopic closure of colon perforation by using a prototype endoscopic suturing device: feasibility and outcome in a porcine model. Gastrointest Endosc. 2006; 64:113–119.

25. Zorron R, Maggioni LC, Pombo L, Oliveira AL, Carvalho GL, Filgueiras M. NOTES transvaginal cholecystectomy: preliminary clinical application. Surg Endosc. 2007 Nov 20

26. Marescaux J, Dallemagne B, Perretta S, Wattiez A, Mutter D, Coumaros D. Surgery without scars: report of transluminal cholecystectomy in a human being. Arch Surg. 2007 Sep;142(9):823-6

27. Decarli LA, Zorron R, Branco A, Lima FC, Tang M, Pioneer SR, Sanseverino JI, Menguer R, Bigolin AV, Gagner M. New Hybrid Approach for NOTES Transvaginal Cholecystectomy: Preliminary Clinical Experience. Surg Innov. 2009 Jun;16(2):181-6

28. Stark M, Benhidjeb T, the New European Surgical Academy (NESA) (2007) Endoscopic surgery in the 21st century. Endosc Rev 12:5–10.

29. Bingener J., Krishnegowda N.K., Michalek J.E. Immunologic parameters during NOTES compared with laparoscopy in a randomized blinded porcine trial. Surg Endosc (2009) 23:178–181.

30. McGee M.F., Schomisch S.J., Marks J.M., DelaneyC.P., Jin J, Williams C, Chak A, Matteson D.T., Andrews J, Ponsky J.L. Late phase TNF-alpha depression in natural orifice translumenal endoscopic surgery (NOTES) peritoneoscopy. Surgery 2008;143:318-28.

31. Decarli L, Zorron R, Branco A, Lima FC, Tang M, Pioneer SR, Zanin I Jr, Schulte AA, Bigolin AV, Gagner M. Natural Orifice Translumenal Endoscopic Surgery (NOTES) Transvaginal Cholecystectomy in a Morbidly Obese Patient. Obes Surg. 2008 Jul;18(7):886-9.

32. Ramos A.C., Zundel N., Galvao Neto M., Maalouf M.. Human hybrid NOTES transvaginal sleeve gastrectomy: initial experience. Surg Obes Relat Dis 2008;4:660–663.

33. Romagnuolo J., Cotton P. Designing Clinical Trials for NOTES. Gastrointest Endoscopy Clin N Am.18 (2008) 371–385

34. Swanstrom L.L., Volckmann E., Hungness E, Soper N.J. Patient attitudes and expectations regarding natural orifice translumenal endoscopic surgery. Surg Endosc (2009) 23:1519–1525.

35. Vettoretto N., Arezzo A. Human natural orifice translumenal endoscopic surgery: on the way to two different philosophies? Surg Endosc. Letter, 2009.

NOTES IN GYNECOLOGY

William Kondo

Alcides José Branco Filho

Aníbal Wood Branco

Rafael William Noda

Monica Tessmann Zomer

Nicolas Bourdel

INTRODUCTION

In recent decades, surgical specialties have experienced advances and changes, being that today's minimally invasive surgical techniques have been adopted to reduce morbidity for patients[1]. The role of laparoscopic surgery in the modern era is already well established. Despite the difficulties in terms of learning curve at the beginning of clinical implementation of the method, currently almost all surgical specialties have adopted this minimally invasive access via as the gold standard technique, resulting in less postoperative pain, shorter hospital stay, faster recovery and better cosmetic results[2-4].

Recently, a new via of minimally invasive surgical approach has been increasingly reported in the literature: transluminal endoscopic surgery by natural orifices (from English NOTES, *Natural Orifice Transluminal Endoscopic Surgery*). It is an access to the abdominal cavity without any incisions in the abdominal wall (surgery without any incisions or *scarless surgery*), with the natural orifices as a gateway into the peritoneal cavity. Thus, an endoscope is inserted into the abdominal cavity through the stomach, vagina, bladder or colon [5].

The first report of this surgical technique was by Gettman et al[6], from the University of Texas in 2002, which demonstrated that transvaginal nephrectomy in experimental animal model was feasible. Two years later, Kalloo et al[7] performed transgastric liver biopsies at Johns Hopkins University. After these initial reports, several researchers have demonstrated the safety of transgastric access to perform tubal ligation[8], cholecystectomy[9], gastrojejunostomy[10], partial hysterectomy with oophorectomy[11,12], splenectomy[13], gastric reduction[14], nephrectomy[15], pancreatectomy[16], all based on studies in experimental pig model.

Since 2007, reports of cholecystectomy[17-19], nephrectomy [20] and tubal ligation[21] using transvaginal NOTES in humans appeared in the literature. More recently, some series of cases have been published[22-24]. Zorron et al[22] reported a multicenter study (16 centers of 9 countries) including 362 patients

73

undergoing transgastric and transvaginal NOTES. The most commonly performed procedures were transvaginal cholecystectomy (66.3%), transvaginal appendectomy (10.2%), transgastric cholecystectomy (8.01%) and transgastric appendectomy (3.87%), corresponding to 88.38% of all procedures.

The global rate of complications was 8.84%, including 5.8% of grades I and II complications and 3.04% for grades III and IV complications. During 14 months of the german record of NOTES[23], 551 patients were operated. The cholecystectomy accounted for 85.3% of all procedures. All procedures were performed in women using transvaginal hybrid technique.

Complications occurred in 3.1% of patients and conversion to laparoscopy or open surgery in 4.9%. In China[24], 43 transvaginal endoscopic cholecystectomies were performed assisted by laparoscopy successfully. No complications intra or postoperative was observed. All patients were satisfied with the aesthetic results. In this chapter, we will discuss about the application of NOTES in gynecology.

STUDIES IN ANIMALS

TRANSGASTRIC ENDOSCOPIC ACCESS

The first gynecological procedures by NOTES were described using the transgastric via. In 2005, Jagannath et al[8] described the first case of transgastric endoscopic peroral tubal ligation in pig model.

Six pigs were submitted to the procedure and the tube of one of the sides was connected using Endoloop by Olympus. Through fluoroscopy, it was confirmed the complete obstruction of the linked tube and preserved patency of the other tube, which served as a control in the study.

All animals survived after surgery. In 2006, Wagh et al[11,12] have published their studies showing that the transgastric endoscopic resection of organs (oophorectomy and partial hysterectomy) was feasible. The surgeries were performed successfully on six female Yorkshire pigs and postoperatively evaluated for 2 weeks without intercurrences. Recently, Freeman et al[25] compared the potential benefits of transgastric NOTES with traditional and laparoscopic surgery. The study included 10 dogs in each group and the variables studied were: complications, surgical stress and postoperative pain. The median operative time was 76, 44 and 35 minutes for NOTES procedures, laparoscopic and open, respectively. All animals survived without complications. The animals from NOTES group showed the greatest increase in serum levels of cortisol in 2 hours, but no difference in glucose concentrations compared with other groups. Serum concentrations of interleukin 6 and C-reactive protein increased significantly in specific times compared with baseline dosages in the NOTES group, but not in the laparoscopic and open surgery groups. Based on cumulative scores of pain, animals in the NOTES group showed less evidence of pain.

TRANSVAGINAL ENDOSCOPIC ACCESS

The retroperitoneal lymphadenectomy by endoscopic transvaginal via in pig model was initially demonstrated by Nassif et al[26] in 2009. They performed three pelvic lymphadenectomy and 3 lymphadenectomy in inter-aortocaval, laterao-aortic and latero-caval regions successfully.

Our Clermont-Ferrand group (CHU Estaing)[27] also evaluated this access via to perform retroperitoneal sentinel lymph node resection in 10 pigs. After injection of blue methylene in the paracervical region (Figures 1A and 1B), the endoscope was introduced through a right lateral colpotomy.

The internal iliac vessels were visualized, followed by identification of bilateral external iliac vessels, aorta and vena cava (Figures 1C to 1E). The sentinel lymph nodes colored in blue were dissected in a blunt manner and removed (Figures 1F to 1I). The mean operative time was 56 minutes and the average number of lymph nodes removed per animal was 1.75. After lymphadenectomy by endoscopic transvaginal access it was performed a laparoscopy which confirmed the removal of 19 from 20 sentinel lymph nodes.

No major complication occurred in the 10 animals. From the 19 sentinel nodes, 11 were localized on the left side and 8 on the right side. Fifteen lymph nodes were obtained from the iliac vessels or from the region of the promontory and 4 of the pre-aortic or aortic lateral region .

Figure 1. Linfonodo Retroperitoneal sentinel lymph node by transvaginal NOTES in animal model. (A and B) Injection of blue methylene in the paracervical region. (C) Visualization of the left kidney. (D) Identification of the right kidney and the vena cava. (E) Bifurcation of the iliac vessels. (F, G, H and I) Removal of the sentinel lymph node colored in blue in the region of the iliac vessels.

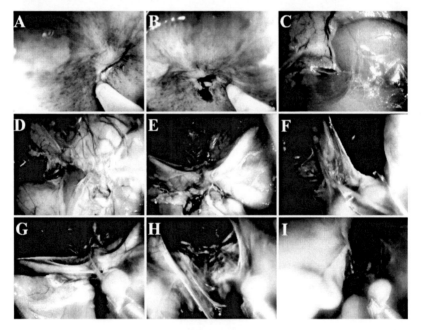

STUDIES IN CORPSES

Until the moment there is no article published in the literature by applying the technique of transvaginal NOTES for gynecological procedures in cadavers. Allemann et al[28] described their experience with pure transvaginal access to exploration of the retroperitoneum in cadavers to simulate possible procedures for nephrectomy, adrenalectomy and pancreatectomy.

The experiments were conducted in three fresh human cadavers, warmed at ambient temperature for 12 hours. The colpotomy was performed on the posterior wall of the vagina, approximately 3 cm proximal to the posterior fornix.

A posterior and left lateral tunnel was created under direct vision, using open and laparoscopic surgical instruments. After entering in the pararectal space, a dual channel endoscope of 12 mm was introduced and the carbon dioxide was insufflated through one of the channels.

The anatomical reference points identified were nerve and artery internal obturator entering in the Alcock's channel, the sacral nerves, the median rectal artery, the external iliac vessels, the left inferior epigastric artery and the inferior pole of the kidney. The access was performed correctly in three corpses until the iliac vessels. In the first case, the frozen tissue prevented the complete dissection untill the kidney. In the other two corpses, the inferior pole of the kidney was clearly visualized. The mean operative time to the access was 52 minutes. Our group of gynecology from Clermont-Ferrand (CHU Estaing) also performed the transvaginal endoscopic access for retroperitoneal evaluation in corpses, but the results were not published. The same surgical steps described before by Allemann et al[28] were performed in three corpses, with an average surgical time of 60 minutes (Figures 2A and 2B).

Figure 2. (A) Retroperitoneal dissection anterior to the sacral bone. (B) Identification of the promontory and the bifurcation of the iliac vessels.

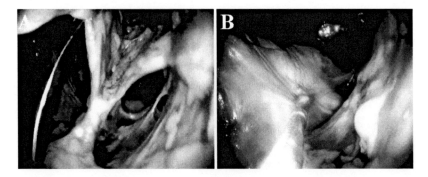

STUDIES IN HUMANS

USE OF RIGID OPTICS

Vaginal access has been used to visualize the pelvic and intra-abdominal organs since from the early 1900s, when it was called culdoscopy. On April 19, 1901, the Russian surgeon Dr. Dmitri von Ott, described for the first time the ventroscopy through colpotomy in Trendelenburg position at the Meeting of the Society of Gynaecology and Obstetrics of Saint Petersburg[29].

TeLinde[30], in 1940, was recognized as the author of one of the first rigid culdoscopy in the United States. Palmer[31] in 1942, introduced transvaginal rigid culdoscopy in the dorsal decubitus.

In the same year, Albert Decker[32] invented what became known as the Decker culdoscope, a rigid instrument with an adjacent lamp to the lens in the distal extremity. Clyman[33], in 1963, used a rigid culdoscope which he performed several procedures, such as lysis of adherences, ovarian biopsies and aspirations of cysts.

In 1999, Watrelot et al[34] described the fertiloscopy, a minimally invasive technique for investigation of female infertility.

It uses a minimally invasive transvaginal access to access the pelvic organs and generally combines the following diagnostic procedures: hidrolaparoscopy (or hidropelviscopy), tubal patency test with methylene blue, salpingoscopy, micro-salpingoscopy and hysteroscopy.

The use of videoscopic instruments inserted by transvaginal via to explore the pelvic peritoneal cavity is feasible and the technique has been applied in thousands of patients with complication rates below 1%[35].

Nohuz et al[36] retrospectively evaluated 229 women with primary or secondary infertility with no pathology to justify a laparoscopy and that could take advantage of a fertiloscopy (Figure 3).

Two hundred and three (88.6%) procedures were successfully performed, revealing injuries in 58 cases (28.6%). Five complications (2.5%) were observed: 2 rectal injuries, two hemorrhagic complications and a postoperative salpingitis. The biggest problem of the rigid endoscope is the inability to explore the whole peritoneal cavity, especially the anterior uterine wall and the peritoneum that covers the surface of the bladder and the broad ligaments[37].

In 2010, Hackethal et al[37] tested two new endoscopes that allow adjustable angles of vision for evaluating women using transvaginal surgery with a rigid endoscope: a 10 mm EndoCAMeleon (Karl Storz, Tuttlingen, Germany) rigid optics that allows angles of vision ranging from 0 to 120 degrees and EndoEYE LTF-VH (Olympus, Hamburg, Germany) which has the flexible tip and reaches an angle of up to 100 degrees. They believed that the use of these new endoscopes would enable the exploitation of all the female pelvis. Four patients with infertility (n=3) and chronic pelvic pain (n=1) were included in the study. They concluded that these new endoscopes do not allow a good quality view of the anterior portion of the pelvis to discard endometriosis or other diseases. For transvaginal surgery with the intention of exploring the pelvic cavity, not rigid endoscopes are not so easy to manipulate as the rigid endoscopes and provide good visualization of the pelvic anatomy.

to inspect the anterior pelvic structures compromises the diagnosis of the patient.

Figure 3. Fertiloscopy. (A) Introduction of optics of fertiloscopy through the posterior fornix. (B) Visualization of the posterior wall of the uterus. (C and D) Left ovary with the presence of slack adherence. (E) Fimbric portion of the left fallopian tube. (F) Fimbric portion of the right fallopian tube . (G and H) Realization of ovarian drilling.

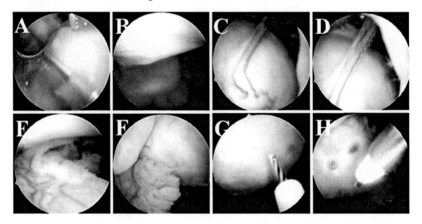

USING FLEXIBLE ENDOSCOPE

In 2009 we performed in Curitiba[21] the first case of bilateral tubal ligation by endoscopic transvaginal access in humans. The patient was positioned in Trendelenburg position and the posterior vaginal fornix was opened to access the peritoneal cavity. A flexible endoscope with dual working channel (Karl Storz Endoskope, Tuttlingen, Germany) was introduced into the pelvic cavity and the pneumoperitoneum was insufflated through a nasogastric probe fixed to the endoscope (Figures 4A and 3B). An uterine manipulator was positioned to facilitate the exposure of the fallopian tubes for the procedure. The fallopian tubes were coagulated and sectioned, and the posterior vaginal fornix was sutured with Vicryl 2-0 (Figures 4C 4I).

Figure 4. Bilateral tubal ligation by transvaginal NOTES. (A) Preparation of endoscope fixing a nasogastric probe to the dual channel endoscope, where carbon dioxide was insufflated to obtain pneumoperitoneum. (B) Opening of the posterior vaginal fornix. (C) Rear view demonstrating the entry area of the endoscope in posterior fornix. (D, E and F) Coagulation of the left fallopian tube. (G, H and I) Coagulation of the right fallopian tube.

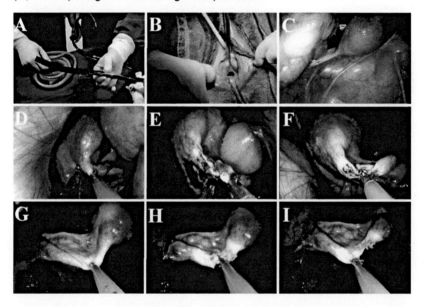

CONTRAINDICATIONS

Transvaginal endoscopic access can not be applied to all patients. There is no study showing which would actually be the relative and absolute contraindications to the procedure, but based on our experience, we quote the following situations as possible contraindications:

- Deep endometriosis: patients with deep endometriosis usually have their lesions located posteriorly to the uterus, either in the uterosacral ligaments, in retrocervical region, or rectovaginal septum. This makes impossible the access to the pelvic cavity through the posterior fornix of the vagina due to the high risk of iatrogenic injuries of adjacent organs during the confection of the access to the pelvic cavity and the presence of intense inflammatory/fibrotic process due to illness, making it difficult the access to the cavity.

- Suspicious adnexal lesions: all suspected adnexal lesions must be approached with the principles of surgical oncology. The precariousness of endoscopic instrumentals still makes that meticulous surgical gestures cannot be performed using this access via. We cannot expose patients to the risk of a possible rupture of a malignant adnexal lesions and consequent contamination of the pelvic cavity with tumor cells.

- Previous pelvic surgery and previous history of pelvic inflammatory disease: previous surgical procedures in the pelvic region and previous episodes of pelvic inflammatory disease may lead to the formation of firm adherences in this region and the instruments currently available to perform transvaginal endoscopic surgery still do not allow the perfect exposure and careful dissection to access the pelvis with large amounts of adherences.

- Complex surgical procedures: the lack of triangulation of instrumentals and the endoscope image obtained through the rear view (upside down and in mirror) do not allow complex surgical gestures to be performed.

DIFFICULTIES

The technical difficulties of performing transvaginal NOTES are already well documented in the literature [19-21] and include:

- Flexibility of conventional endoscopes: limits the control of instruments during surgery.

- Lack of triangulation: as the instruments are inserted through the two working channels of the flexible endoscope, they reach the peritoneal cavity in parallel, which limits the movements of the surgeon.

- Lack of stability of the endoscope: the endoscope does not remain standing in the peritoneal cavity during surgery, so constantly the ideal surgical exposure is lost. Moreover, the movement of the instruments moves in conjunction the endoscope, which facilitates the loss of the surgical field.

- Rear view: pelvic surgery is performed with rear view, which implies an upside-down image and inverted, making the notion of movement of the instruments and even the endoscope difficult. It is not always obtained a front view with rear view; and often lateral view is obtained, which makes the procedure more arduous.

TRANSVAGINAL ENDOSCOPIC ACCESS – FOR AND AGAINST

The transvaginal endoscopic access presents several potential advantages: it is well accepted by patients because it leaves no scars on the abdomen, it reproduces laparoscopic surgery, it is associated with minimal morbidity, it allows visualization of all pelvic anatomy, the postoperative pain is minimal and the postoperative recovery time is reduced. It also prevents hernias in the trocar orifices, and may, even, reduce the formation of intra-abdominal adherences [38,39].

The disadvantages of the method include: the impossibility of application in all patients, it needs long learning curve and prolonged time of sexual abstinence after the procedure to complete vaginal cicatrization.

FINAL CONSIDERATIONS

A transluminal endoscopic surgery by natural orifices using the vagina as point of entry to the peritoneal cavity is a quite promising technique and several surgical procedures have been performed using this via. With the development of new instrumentals and platforms that facilitate the handling and stabilization of flexible endoscopes, this surgical approach tends to have a major clinical application in the future.

REFERENCES

1. Branco AW, Branco Filho AJ, Noda RW, George MA, Camargo AHLA, Kondo W. New minimally invasive surgical approaches: transvaginal and transumbilical. Braz J Video-Sur 2008; 1(1):29-36.

2. Kondo W, Rangel M, Tirapelle RA, Garcia MA, Bahten LCV, Laux GL, Smaniotto B. Emprego da laparoscopia em mulheres com dor abdominal aguda. Rev Bras Videocir 2006; 4(1):3-8.

3. Jin C, Hu Y, Chen XC, Zheng FY, Lin F, Zhou K, Chen FD, Gu HZ. Laparoscopic versus open myomectomy--a meta-analysis of randomized controlled trials. Eur J Obstet Gynecol Reprod Biol. 2009 Jul;145(1):14-21. Epub 2009 Apr 23.

4. Keus F, Gooszen HG, van Laarhoven CJ. Open, small-incision, or laparoscopic cholecystectomy for patients with symptomatic cholecystolithiasis. An overview of Cochrane Hepato-Biliary Group reviews. Cochrane Database Syst Rev. 2010 Jan 20;(1):CD008318.

5. de la Fuente SG, Demaria EJ, Reynolds JD, Portenier DD, Pryor AD. New developments in surgery: Natural Orifice Transluminal Endoscopic Surgery (NOTES). Arch Surg. 2007 Mar;142(3):295-7.

6. Gettman MT, Lotan Y, Napper CA, Cadeddu JA. Transvaginal laparoscopic nephrectomy: development and feasibility in the porcine model. Urology. 2002 Mar;59(3):446-50.

7. Kalloo AN, Singh VK, Jagannath SB, Niiyama H, Hill SL, Vaughn CA, Magee CA, Kantsevoy SV. Flexible transgastric peritoneoscopy: a novel approach to diagnostic and therapeutic interventions in the peritoneal cavity. Gastrointest Endosc. 2004 Jul;60(1):114-7.

8. Jagannath SB, Kantsevoy SV, Vaughn CA, Chung SS, Cotton PB, Gostout CJ, Hawes RH, Pasricha PJ, Scorpio DG, Magee CA, Pipitone LJ, Kalloo AN. Peroral transgastric endoscopic ligation of fallopian tubes with long-term survival in a porcine model. Gastrointest Endosc. 2005 Mar;61(3):449-53.

9. Park PO, Bergström M, Ikeda K, Fritscher-Ravens A, Swain P. Experimental studies of transgastric gallbladder surgery: cholecystectomy and cholecystogastric anastomosis (videos). Gastrointest Endosc. 2005 Apr;61(4):601-6.

10. Kantsevoy SV, Jagannath SB, Niiyama H, Chung SS, Cotton PB, Gostout CJ, Hawes RH, Pasricha PJ, Magee CA, Vaughn CA, Barlow D, Shimonaka H, Kalloo AN. Endoscopic gastrojejunostomy with survival in a porcine model. Gastrointest Endosc. 2005 Aug;62(2):287-92.

14. Kantsevoy SV, Hu B, Jagannath SB, Isakovich NV, Chung SS, Cotton PB, Gostout CJ, Hawes RH, Pasricha PJ, Nakajima Y, Kawashima K, Kalloo AN. Technical feasibility of endoscopic gastric reduction: a pilot study in a porcine model. Gastrointest Endosc. 2007 Mar;65(3):510-3.

15. Lima E, Rolanda C, Pêgo JM, Henriques-Coelho T, Silva D, Osório L, Moreira I, Carvalho JL, Correia-Pinto J. Third-generation nephrectomy by natural orifice transluminal endoscopic surgery. J Urol. 2007 Dec;178(6):2648-54. Epub 2007 Oct 22.

16. Matthes K, Yusuf TE, Willingham FF, Mino-Kenudson M, Rattner DW, Brugge WR. Feasibility of endoscopic transgastric distal pancreatectomy in a porcine animal model. Gastrointest Endosc. 2007 Oct;66(4):762-6.

17. Marescaux J, Dallemagne B, Perretta S, Wattiez A, Mutter D, Coumaros D. Surgery without scars: report of transluminal cholecystectomy in a human being. Arch Surg. 2007 Sep;142(9):823-6; discussion 826-7.

18. Zorrón R, Filgueiras M, Maggioni LC, Pombo L, Lopes Carvalho G, Lacerda Oliveira A. NOTES. Transvaginal cholecystectomy: report of the first case. Surg Innov. 2007 Dec;14(4):279-83.

19. Branco Filho AJ, Noda RW, Kondo W, Kawahara N, Rangel M, Branco AW. Initial experience with hybrid transvaginal cholecystectomy. Gastrointest Endosc. 2007 Dec;66(6):1245-8.

20. Branco AW, Branco Filho AJ, Kondo W, Noda RW, Kawahara N, Camargo AA, Stunitz LC, Valente J, Rangel M. Hybrid transvaginal nephrectomy. Eur Urol. 2008 Jun;53(6):1290-4. Epub 2007 Nov 5.

21. Kondo W, Noda RW, Branco AW, Rangel M, Branco Filho AJ. Transvaginal endoscopic tubal sterilization. J Laparoendosc Adv Surg Tech A. 2009 Feb;19(1):59-61.

22. Zorron R, Palanivelu C, Galvão Neto MP, Ramos A, Salinas G, Burghardt J, DeCarli L, Henrique Sousa L, Forgione A, Pugliese R, Branco AJ, Balashanmugan TS, Boza C, Corcione F, D'Avila Avila F, Arturo Gómez N, Galvão Ribeiro PA, Martins S, Filgueiras M, Gellert K, Wood Branco A, Kondo W, Inacio Sanseverino J, de Sousa JA, Saavedra L, Ramírez E, Campos J, Sivakumar K, Rajan PS, Jategaonkar PA, Ranagrajan M, Parthasarathi R, Senthilnathan P, Prasad M, Cuccurullo D, Müller V. International multicenter trial on clinical natural orifice surgery--NOTES IMTN study: preliminary results of 362 patients. Surg Innov. 2010 Jun;17(2):142-58.

23. Lehmann KS, Ritz JP, Wibmer A, Gellert K, Zornig C, Burghardt J, Büsing M, Runkel N, Kohlhaw K, Albrecht R, Kirchner TG, Arlt G, Mall JW, Butters M, Bulian DR, Bretschneider J, Holmer C, Buhr HJ. The German registry for natural orifice translumenal endoscopic surgery: report of the first 551 patients. Ann Surg. 2010 Aug;252(2):263-70.

24. Niu J, Song W, Yan M, Fan W, Niu W, Liu E, Peng C, Lin P, Li P, Khan AQ. Transvaginal laparoscopically assisted endoscopic cholecystectomy: preliminary clinical results for a series of 43 cases in China. Surg Endosc. 2010 Oct 7. [Epub ahead of print]

25. Freeman LJ, Rahmani EY, Al-Haddad M, Sherman S, Chiorean MV, Selzer DJ, Snyder PW, Constable PD. Comparison of pain and postoperative stress in dogs undergoing natural orifice transluminal endoscopic surgery, laparoscopic, and open oophorectomy. Gastrointest Endosc. 2010 Aug;72(2):373-80. Epub 2010 May 26.

26. Nassif J, Zacharopoulou C, Marescaux J, Wattiez A. Transvaginal extraperitoneal lymphadenectomy by Natural Orifices Transluminal Endoscopic Surgery (NOTES) technique in porcine model: feasibility and survival study. Gynecol Oncol. 2009 Feb;112(2):405-8. Epub 2008 Nov 20.

27. Bourdel N, Kondo W, Botchorishvili R, Poincloux L, Niro J, Rabischong B, Jardon K, Pouly JL, Mage G, Canis M. Assessment of sentinel nodes for gynecologic malignancies by natural orifices transluminal endoscopic surgery (NOTES): preliminary report. Gynecol Oncol. 2009 Dec;115(3):367-70. Epub 2009 Oct 3.

28. Allemann P, Perretta S, Asakuma M, Dallemagne B, Marescaux J. NOTES new frontier: Natural orifice approach to retroperitoneal disease. World J Gastrointest Surg. 2010 May 27;2(5):157-64.

29. Von Ott D. Die Beleuchtung der Bauchhohle (Ventroskopie) als Methode bei Vaginaler Coeliotomie. Abl Gynakol. 1902; 231:817-23.

30. Frenkel DA, Greene BA, Siegler SL. Technical improvements in culdoscopic examination. Am J Obstet Gynecol. 1952; 64:1303-9.

31. Brosens I, Campo R, Puttemans P, Gordts S. Transvaginal laparoscopy. Clin Obstet Gynecol. 2003 Mar;46(1):117-22.

32. Decker A. Culdoscopy. Am J Obstet Gynecol. 1952; 63:854-9.

33. Clyman MJ. A new panculdoscope – diagnostic, photographic, and operative aspects. Obstet Gynecol. 1963; 21:343-8.

34. Watrelot A, Dreyfus JM, Andine JP. Evaluation of the performance of fertiloscopy in 160 consecutive infertile patients with no obvious pathology. Hum Reprod. 1999; 14:707-11.

35. Gordts S, Campo R, Puttemans P, Gordts Sy, Brosens I. Transvaginal access: a safe technique for tubo-ovarian exploration in infertility? Review of the literature. Gynecol Surg. 2008; 5(3):187–91.

36. Nohuz E, Pouly JL, Bolandard F, Rabischong B, Jardon K, Cotte B, Rivoire C, Mage G. Fertiloscopy: Clermont-Ferrand's experiment. Gynecol Obstet Fertil. 2006 Oct;34(10):894-9. Epub 2006 Sep 18.

37. Hackethal A, Ionesi-Pasacica J, Eskef K, Oehmke F, Münstedt K, Tinneberg HR. Transvaginal NOTES with semi-rigid and rigid endoscopes that allow adjustable viewing angles. Arch Gynecol Obstet. 2010 Mar 25.

38. Dubcenco E, Assumpcao L, Dray X, Gabrielson KL, Ruben DS, Pipitone LJ, Donatelli G, Krishnamurty DM, Baker JP, Marohn MR, Kalloo AN. Adhesion formation after peritoneoscopy with liver biopsy in a survival porcine model: comparison of laparotomy, laparoscopy, and transgastric natural orifice transluminal endoscopic surgery (NOTES). Endoscopy. 2009 Nov;41(11):971-8. Epub 2009 Oct 28.

39. Tonouchi H, Ohmori Y, Kobayashi M, Kusunoki M. Trocar site hernia. Arch Surg. 2004 Nov;139(11):1248-56.

LESS – LAPAROENDOSCOPIC SINGLE SITE SURGERY

James Skinovsky

Marcus Vinícius Dantas de Campos Martins

Djalma Ernesto Coelho Neto

Mauricio Chibata

Rogério Augusto Cavalliére

INTRODUCTION

In 1987, by the hands of the French surgeons Mouret and Perissat, began the videosurgery, one of the greatest revolutions in the history of surgical art, comparable to major advances of the past such as the discovery of anesthesia and antibiotic therapy. Minimally invasive surgery has brought less suffering, less severe metabolic changes and faster recovery for patients, disseminating itself through the operating rooms of the world quickly and enthusiastically.

The permanent improvement of optical equipment, as well as the instrumental used in videosurgery, has allowed that increasingly complex operations could be performed by the method minimally invasive.

The permanent improvement of optical equipment, as well as the instrument used in videosurgery, has allowed increasingly complex operations could be determined by the method minimally invasive.

Several parallel technologies and new approaches have emerged in the wave of surgical revolution in progress, such as surgery at a distance (or telesurgery), robotics applied to surgery, teaching through internet, virtual reality, surgery by natural orifices (NOTES) and surgery by single access or LESS – LaparoEndoscopic Single Site Surgery .

It is appropriate here to make the differentiation between the surgery by single incision, where several trocars are inserted into an incision of varying size and the surgery by single access, performed with a defined size of the incision, with the introduction of a single multiport trocar.

NOTES is still in the field of experimentation, while LESS is on a step up, being prepared for immediate use.

This chapter, the available platforms are going to be discussed, using the current practice and the results already measured in this approach that, it is certainly an advance for videosurgery and for those who need it.

LESS - THE EVOLUTION

Kaloo[1] published in 2004, for the first time, a study versing about translumenal access to the organs of the abdominal cavity using transgastric approach in pigs, whose method is now known as NOTES (*Natural Orifice Translumenal Endoscopic Surgery*). Since then, several researchers around the world has been developing studies on the development of new equipment and instrumental for this approach, seeking to define its feasibility and practical application.

In 2005, in New York city, members of *American Society of Gastrointestinal Endoscopy* (ASGE) and *Society of American Gastrointestinal and Endoscopic Surgeons* (SAGES) have met, whose group was then called NOSCAR (*Natural Orifices Surgery Consortium for Assessment and Research*), producing a document called *White Paper,* which defined lines of research, potential benefits and priorities.[2,3]

Dantas Martins et al[4] published, in 2006, a study dealing with the use of the transgastric approach in pigs, emphasizing that barriers must be overcome, then this new technology could have massive practical application .

The training and demand for new workstations, as well as access to the abdominal cavity, closure of the stomach and other hollow viscera, the infectious potential, the development of new and necessary equipment and the difficulty of spatial orientation with the use of common endoscopes emerged as difficulties for the development of translumenal surgery and still must be overcome to transform NOTES in reality, in daily clinical and surgical application.

Wheeless is credited as being the first to use the principles of surgery by single access, in 1969, performing tubal ligation [5].

In 1996, Kala[6] published a study suggesting a single trans-umbilical approach for appendectomy, video assisted and with the appendix removed in an extra-corporeal way. In the following year Navarra[7] et al. described cholecystectomy performed through two 10 mm trocars, introduced through umbilical via .

LESS then entered in a period of latency, resurfacing in 2007, when Zhu published his first experience using the umbilical scar as an only access to the peritoneal cavity, having performed a fenestration of hepatic cyst, followed by abdominal exploration and appendectomy, designating this new technique as *Transumbilical Endoscopic Surgery* (TUES)[8]. The author used standard flexible endoscope and instrumental introduced by its work channels.

In 2008, again Zhu[9] et al. published a study describing TUES new cases: two cases of fenestration of hepatic cysts, six cholecystectomies and nine appendectomies, using a trocar with three working channels.

Palanivelu[10] et al., Indian authors have published, in 2008, a study describing eight trans-umbilical appendectomy, using standard flexible endoscope. The authors consider the technique as a preparatory step for NOTE.

In this same year Desai et al[11] reported pioneers cases of nephrectomy and pieloplasty, using a three channels trocar named R-Port[TM]; adrenalectomy was effected by Castellucci[12] and one case of right colectomy by single surgical access was also described, by Bucher et al[13].

Surgical treatment of morbid obesity was successfully completed by Saber et al[14] and also by Reavis et al.[15], through *sleeve gastrectomy* and, in 2009, Teixeira et al. published series of ten adjustable gastric band operations by single umbilical incision[16] and Saber et al[17] reported the first case of Gastric Bypass in Roux Y, by multiport trocar.

In 2009 Zhu et al[18] described the new surgical series by single transumbilical access, with three cases of fenestration of hepatic cyst, 10 appendectomies and 26 cholecystectomy using a three channel trocar. In this year Podolsky reported five gastrotomy by single access, in patients who could not receive endoscopic percutaneous gastrostomy[19].

Recently Cadeddu et al[20] and Dominguez et al.[21] reported the use of magnets, in order to expand the visual field and facilitate the mobility of the instrumental in nephrectomy, appendectomy and cholecystectomy by single trocar. Also in 2009, Busch et al.[22] reported a case of gastrojejunostomy with intracorporeal anastomosis, through single trans-umbilical trocar and Targarona[23] and collaborators described the technique of splenectomy. In 2010 Ishikawa et al[24] reported the performance of laparoscopic hernioplasty by TAPP technique, and Agrawal et al[25] performed the treatment for hernia by TEP technique, both with multiport trocar.

Also in 2010 was created LESSCAR[26], a consortium with the aim of leveraging the research and development of equipment needed to surgery by single trocar, compiling its advantages and problems to solve.

As seen, surgeries in several operative areas have been performed by the approach of single surgical access, besides those already reported, such as varied urologic surgery[27, 28] (nephrectomy, radical prostatectomy, adrenalectomy, radical cystectomy, nephrectomy in transplant donor etc..) and splenectomy[37].

All data indicate that surgery by single transumbilical via is technically feasible, being that the varied terminology has been proposed to designate it, besides the already mentioned TUES, such as SILS – *Single Incision Laparoscopic Surgery*, SPA – *Single-Port Access*, e-NOTES - *Embryonic Natural Orifice Transumblical Endoscopic Surgery*, LESS - *Laparo-Endoscopic Single-Site* , NOTUS – *Natural Orifice Trans-Umbilical Surgery*, OPUS – *One-Port Umbilical Surgery* and SITRACC- *Single Trocar Access*[30] . In our opinion, the terms that best fit this new approach are SITRACC and SPA, as it is a procedure performed by equipment that allows access through a single via, not a single incision not even through embryonic arguably orifice, not even obligatorily through umbilical via, because several operations with this technique do not necessarily use this route, as nephrectomy.

Several models of multichannel trocar has been developed by companies around the world, as SITRACC® (Edlo, Brasil), Single-site Laparoscopic Access System® (Ethicon Endo-Surgery), GelPort® (Applied Medical, USA) , TriPort or R-Port System® (Advanced Surgical Concepts, Ireland), X-Cone® e Endocone® (Karl-Storz, Germany), SILS® (Covidien, USA), AirSeal® (SurgiQuest, USA) and SPIDER System® (TransEnterix,USA)[29] all of them assuming the use of a multichannel trocar and curved, flexible and/or articulated instrumental (Figures 1, 2, 3, 4, 5, 6, 7 and 8) - Table 1.

Figures 1 and 2 – SITRACC® – Single Trocar Access, Edlo, Brazil

Figures 3 and 4 - TriPort ®or R-port®, Advanced Surgical Concepts, Wicklow, Ireland - Courtesy – Dr Manoel Galvão Neto, in: Galvão Neto M, Ramos A, Campos J. Single port laparoscopy Access surgery. Tech Gastrointest Endosc 2009;11(2):84-94.

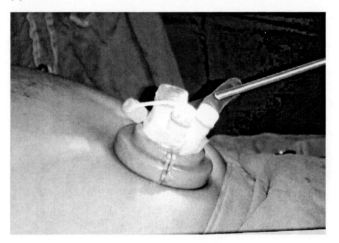

Figure 5 - Single Site Laparoscopic Access System

Ethicon Endo-Surgery, Inc., Cincinnati, OH, USA. Courtesy Dr Manoel Galvão Neto –in:Galvão Neto M, Ramos A, Campos J. Single port laparoscopy Access surgery. Tech Gastrointest Endosc 2009;11(2):84-94.

Figure 6 - SILS™ Port Multiple Access Port, Covidien, Norwalk, CT, USA. Courtesy – Dr Manoel Galvão Neto, in:Galvão Neto M, Ramos A, Campos J. Single port laparoscopy Access surgery. Tech Gastrointest Endosc 2009;11(2):84-94.

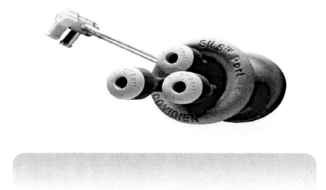

Figures 7 and 8 - X-CONE®, Karl Storz, Tuttlingen, Germany. Notice the platform with curved instruments. Courtesy – Dr Manoel Galvão Neto, in:

Galvão Neto M, Ramos A, Campos J. Single port laparoscopy Access surgery. Tech Gastrointest Endosc 2009;11(2):84-94.

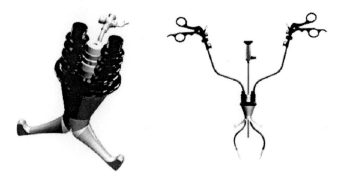

Table 1 Comparison among the platforms of surgery by single access. Courtesy: Dr Manoel Galvão et al.

Plataforms S-Port	Company/Introduction Method		Size of the incision	Entry channels -mm
SSLAS	Ethicon/Open		2,5-3 cm	2 models –
				1 of 15+2 of 5
				2 of 12+2 of 5
Tri-Port ou R-Port	Olympus/ puncture	Closed	2-3cm	2 model –
				1 of 10 + 2 of 5
				2 of 12 and 2 and 5
SILS	Covidien/Open		3-4 cm	2 variations –
				1 of 12 and 2 of 5
				2 of 12 and 1 of 5
X-Cone	Storz/Open		2,5-5 cm	2 models –
				1 of 12 and 2 of 5
SITRACC	Edlo/Open		2,5-4 cm	2 of 12 and 6 of 5
				3 models
				4 of 5
				1 of 10 and 3 of 5
				1 of 13 and 3 of 5

In 2007, began in Brazil the pioneering attempt to develop a platform for surgery by single access, called SITRACC ® (Single Trocar Access, Edlo, Brazil), consisting of trocar with four working channels (three of 5 mm and one of 10 mm or four of 5 mm); flexible and/or articulated instrumental was specially developed for this approach (Fig. 9 a, b, c, d). After studies in experimental animals, in the following year was published the first case of SITRACC cholecystectomy performed in humans [30,31].

Figure 9 – Flexible/articulated instrumental-SITRACC ® (Edlo, Brazil) 9a Dissector Clamp with distal articulation, 9b Hook with distal articulation, 9c curved scissors and 9d demonstration of the articulation of the distal Hook

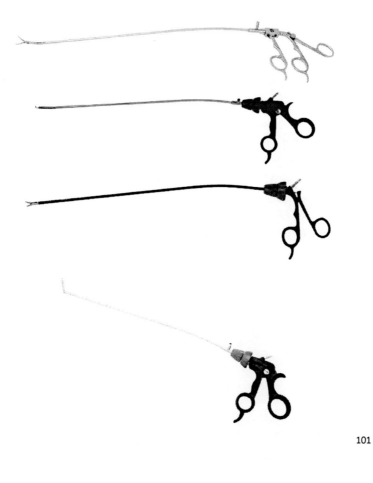

Figure 10 – Grasper from SITRACC totally flexible (Edlo, Brazil)

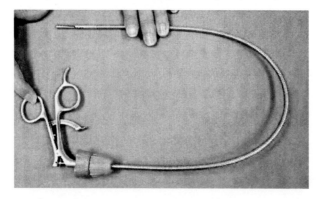

A multicenter study[32] began in 2008, with the participation of nine Brazilian surgery services, in several cities, culminating with the performance of 81 SITRACC ® cholecystectomies, as observed in Table 2.

Table 2 – SITRACC Cholecystectomy - Brazilian multicentric study

Team	Cities	N of patients
James Skinovsky/Marcus V Dantas	Curitiba - PR	41
Almino Ramos/Manuel Galvão	São Paulo - SP	09

The mean operative time was 68 minutes and the average age of patients was 48 years, being 52 females and 29 males; ten surgeries needed to place an extra trocar, in right hypochondrium, due to technical difficulties. Three cholecystectomies were converted to conventional videolaparoscopy, two due to difficult vesicular infundibulum, by acute cholecystitis, and one by morbid obesity, with difficult installation of the trocar and instrumental.

In our experience with the SITRACC approach, 150 cholecystectomies were performed, and, of these, eleven needed an additional portal of 5 mm and, on six opportunities, it was required the full conversion for what we conventionally call conventional videolaparoscopy (all by " difficult infundibulum").

CONSIDERATIONS

The laparoscopic technique is based primarily on the principles of traction and counter-traction, allowing triangulation of forces from two different points. According to Galvão Neto et al[33] when inserting laparoscopic instruments through a single portal, triangulation is impaired, as well as the visualization of the operative field, remaining these disposed in a single axis. To counterbalance this effect is necessary curved and/or articulated instrumental , such as those developed by Edlo (SITRACC, Brasil), Covidien (Roticulator, USA) and Real Hand (USA).

The main difficulty to be overcome is that due to the need to work on single axis of action, with the instruments disposed in parallel; the attempt to meet this challenge is represented by the mentioned development of flexible and/or articulated instrumental at its distal extremity, enabling triangulation, albeit limited when compared to conventional laparoscopic surgery[33,34,35].

The internal movement of the instrumental, even adapted for LESS, is arduous, and must be remembered that, when moving a single instrument, the

103

whole tends to move in a single axis, requiring a trained team and experienced in the technique, so that the visual field is not changed (Figure 11). The use of optics with angulation of at least 30 degrees is strongly recommended, providing better visualization of the operative object.

Figure 11 – Instruments Disposition - SITRACC ®

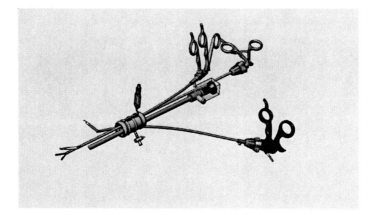

It should be also consider that, with the technical evolution of the equipment, the facilitated availability of the cables of light source, with output of 180 degrees, from optics, will compete, to lower external collision of the instrumental.

Both sutures and internal nodes are equally hampered, and we recommend the use of external nodes and endoloops. Trocars that allow the passage of staplers are being developed, and may, in the near future, facilitate the performance of resection surgeries, such as bariatric surgery.

The training requires patience and time, since, as shown, it is not a simple variation of laparoscopy and yes a new approach, practice in courses with experimental animals, as well as in simulations (Figure 12), (www.lapsurg . com.br) are essential for posterior good results, in human surgery.

The advantages of LESS, in relation to NOTES, vary in range from maintaining the principle of so-called Scarless Surgery ie minimal or no scarring (Figures 13 A, B and C), through the provided vision, next of which the surgeon is already used to, in videolaparoscopic surgical procedures, reaching at a minimum risk of infection (theoretically equal to the conventional laparoscopy, or less, since there is only one portal).

Figure 12 – Simulator for training in Surgery by Single Portal

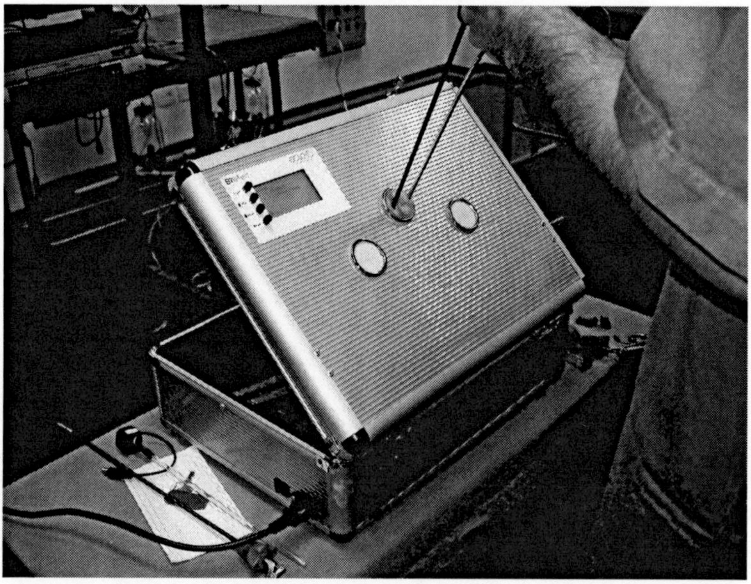

Figures 13 A, 13 B and 13C – Aesthetic result - Immediate postoperative, 7 and
30 days post-cholecystectomy SITRACC

A

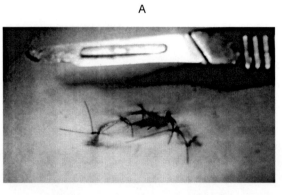

B

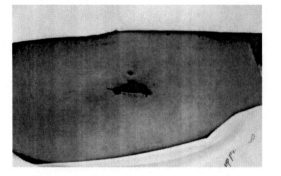

C

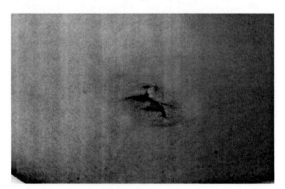

In preliminary work, 10 Single Trocar Access cholecystectomies were compared by our team with 10 identical procedures performed by conventional videolaparoscopy; it were studied inflammatory markers C-reactive protein and erythrocyte sedimentation rate - ESR (measured pre-operatively, 6 and 12 hours after the procedure), besides the painful intensity, through a visual scale applied 1, 12, and 24 hours after the operation.

The results indicated, after appropriate statistical analysis, that there was no significant difference in relation to ESR and that C-reactive protein showed results significantly lower in 6 hs measuring, in the SITRACC group. The pain measured was not statistically lower in either group. On the contrary, the study of Tsimoyiannis et al [36]., in 2010, it was verified less pain in the first postoperatively 24 hours, compared to conventional videolaparoscopic cholecystectomy with the same procedure, performed by a single incision.

In another parallel study, 20 patients have completed one year of the procedure were compared to 20 other patients with similar postoperative period after the performance of conventional videocholecystectomies, being applied the Brazilian version of the SF-36 quality of life questionnaire. The results indicated that it was not significantly different in both groups. Also there was no difference in relation to the occurrence of hernia at the site of trocar.

Although we need large comparative series between surgical procedures by single access and those performed by videosurgical approach now said conventional.

While these are not performed, published and validated by the worldwide surgical community, we can only guess what the preliminary data allow to view, that LESS is an excellent choice to performe minimally invasive procedures, with all the advantages that these actions carry with them, from aesthetics to milder pain and faster return to routine activities of the patient.

The LESS access procedures must be remembered as part of a surgical armamentarium, passing through open surgery, videosurgery and eventually by NOTES, according to published studies in the future allow us to relate, each patient is unique, as well as their disease. It is up to surgeons to determine the best method of approach that will bring a mix of security, best operative and aesthetic result.

REFERENCES

1. Kallo NA, Sibgh VK, Jagannath SB, Niiyama H, Vaugh CA, Magee CA, Kantsevoy SV. Flexible transgastric peritoneoscopy: a novel approach to diagnostic and therapeutic interventions. Gastrointest Endosc 2004; 60: 114-

2. ASGE/SAGES Working Group on Natural Orifice Translumenal Endoscopic Surgery White Paper. Gastrointest Endosc 2006;63:199-203.

3. Giday SA, Kantsevoy SV, Kaloo AN. Principle and history of natural orifice translumenal endoscopic surgery (NOTES). Minim Invasive Ther Allied Technol 2006;15:373-377.

4. Martins MVDC, Coelho DE, Coelho JF, Rios M. Inicial experience with natural orifices transluminal endoscopic surgery. Rev Bras Videocir 2006;4(2): 75-77.

5. Wheeless CR. A rapid, inexpence and effective method of surgical sterilization by laparoscopy. J Reprod Med 1969;5:255.

6. Kala Z: A modified technic in laparoscopy-assisted appendectomy--a transumbilical approach through a single port. Rozhl Chir 1996;75(1):15-

7. Navarra G: One-wound laparoscopic cholecystectomy. Br J Surg 1997;84(5):695.

8. Zhu JF. Scarless endoscopic surgery: NOTES or TUES. Surg Endosc 2007;21:1898-1899.

9. Zhu JF, Hu H, Ma YZ, Xu MZ, Li F. Transumbilical endoscopic surgery: a preliminary clinical report. Surg Endosc [periodical online] 2008; Available from: URL:http//www.springerlink.com/content [consulted on 02/01/2009].

10. Papanivelu C, Rajan PS, Rangarajan M, Parthasarathi R, Senthilnathan P, Praveenraj P. Transumbilical endoscopic appendectomy in humans: on the road to NOTES: a prospective study. J Laparoendosc & Advanced Surg Tech 2008; 18(4): 579-582.

11. Desai MM, Rao PP, Aron M, Haber GP, Desai M, Mishra S, Kaouk JH, Gill IS. Scarless single port transumbilical nephrectomy and pyeloplasty: first clinical report. Brit J Urology 2008; 101: 83-88.

12. Castellucci SA, Curcillo PG, Ginsberg PC, et al: Single-port access adrenalectomy. J Endourol 2008; 22:1573–1576.

13. Bucher P, Pugin F, Morel P. Single port access laparoscopic right hemicolectomy. Int J Colorectal Dis 2008; 23:1013-1016.

14. Saber AA, Elgamal MH, Itawi EA, Rao AJ. Single incision laparoscopic sleeve gastrectomy (SILS): a novel technique. Obes Surg 2008; 18:1338-1342.

15. Reavis KM, Hinojosa MW, Smith BR, et al: Single laparoscopic-incision transabdominal surgery sleeve gastrectomy. Obes Surg 2008; 18(11):1492–1494.

16. Teixeira J, McGill K, Binenbaum S, Forrester G. Laparoscopic single-site surgery for placement of na adjustable gastric band: initial experience. Surg Endosc 2009; 23:1409-1414.

17. Saber AA, El-Ghazaly T, Minnick D. Single port access transumbilical laparoscopic Roux-en-Y gastric bypass using the SILS port: first reported case. Surg Innov 2009;on line - sri.sagepub.com

18. Zhu JF, Hu H, Ma YZ, Xu MZ, Li F. Transumbilical endoscopic surgery: a preliminary clinical report. Surg Endosc 2009; 23:813-817.

19. Podolsy ER, Rottman SJ, Curcillo PG. Single Port Access (SPA^{TM}) gastrostomy tube in patients unable to receive percutaneous endoscopic gastrostomy placement. Surg Endosc 2009; 23:1142-1145.

20. Cadeddu J, Fernandez R, Desai M, Bergs R, Tracy C, Tang SJ, Rao P, Desai M, Scott D. Novel magnetically guided intra-abdominal camera to facilitate laparoendoscopic single-site surgery: initial human experience. Surg Endosc 2009; 23:1894-1899.

21. Dominguez G, Durand L, De Rosa J, Danguise E, Arozamena C, Ferraina PA. Retraction and triangulation with neodymiun magnetic fórceps for single-port laparoscopic cholecystectomy. Surg Endosc 2009; 23:1660-1666.

22. Busher P, Pugin F, Morel P. Transumbilical single-incision laparoscopic intracorporeal anastomosis for gastrojejunostomy: case report. Surg Endosc 2009; 23:1667-1670.

23. Targarona EM, Balaque C, Martinez C, Pallares L, Estalella L, Trias M. Single-Port Access: a feasible alternative to conventional laparoscopic splenectomy. Surg Innov 2009; on line - sri.sagepub.com.

24. Ishikawa N, Kawaguchi M, Shimizu S, Matsunoki A, Inaki N, watanabe G. Single-incision laparoscopic hernioplasty with the assistance of the Radius Surgical System. Surg Endosc 2010; 24:730-731.

25. Agrawal S, Shaw A, Soon Y. Single-Port laparoscopic totally extraperitoneal inguinal hernia repair with the TriPort system: initial experience. Surg Endosc 2010; 24:952-956.

26. Gill IS, Advincula P, Aron M, Caddedu J, Canes D, Curcillo P, Desai M, Evanko J, Falcone T, Fazio V, Gettman M, Gumbs A, Haber G, Kaouk J, Kim F, King S, Ponsky J, Remzi F, Rivas H, Rosemurgy A, Ross S, Schauer P, Sotelo R, Speranza J, Eweeney J, Teixeira J.Consensus statement of the consortium for laparoendoscopic single-site surgery. Surg Endosc 2010; 24:762-768.

27. Kaouk JH, Haber GP, Goel RK. Single-port laparoscopic surgery in urology: initial experience. Urology 2008; 71(1):3-6.

28. Rané A, Rao P, Rao Pr. Single-Port-Access Nephrectomy and other laparoscopic urologic procedures using a novel laparoscopic port (R-Port). Urology 2008; 72:260-264.

29. Pryor AD, Tushar J, DiBernardo L. Single-port cholecystectomy with the TransEnterix SPIDER: simple and safe. Surg Endosc 2010; 24:917-923.

30. Dantas MVDC, Skinovsky J, Coelho DE, Torres MF. SITRACC – Single Trocar Access: a new device for a new surgical approach. Bras J Vide-Surg 2008; 1(2):60-63.

31. Dantas MVDC, Skinovsky J, Coelho DE. Colecistectomia videolaparoscópica por trocarte único (SITRACC): Uma nova opção. Rev Col Bras Surg 2009; 36(2):177-179.

32. Martins MVD, Skinovsky J, Coelho DE, Ramos A, Galvão Neto MP, Rodrigues J, de Carli L, Cavazolla, LT, Campos J, Thuller F, Brunetti A. Cholecystectomy by single trocar access – SITRACC: The first multicenter study. Surg Innov 2009;Dez – on line - sri.sagepub.com.

33. Galvão Neto M, Ramos A, Campos J. Single port laparoscopy Access surgery. Tech Gastrointest Endosc 2009;11(2):84-94.

34. Zhu JF. Which term is better: SILS, SPA, LESS, E-NOTES or TUES? Surg Endosc 2009; 23:1164-1165.

35. Romanelli JR, Earle DB. Single-port laparoscopic surgery: an overview. Surg Endosc 2009;23:1419-1427.

36. Tsimoyiannis EC, Tsimogiannis KE, Pappas-Gogos G, Farantos C, Benetatos N, Mavridou P, Manataki A. Different pain scores in single transumbilical incision laparoscopic cholecystectomy versus classic laparoscopic cholecystectomy: a randomized controled Trial. Surg Endosc 2010;24:1842-1848.

37. Targarona EM, Pallares JL, Balague C, Luppi CR, Marinello F, P Hernández,Martìnez C, Trias M. Single incision approuch for splenic diseases: a preliminary report on a series of 8 cases. Surg Endosc 2010;24:2236-2240.

SITRACC CHOLECYSTECTOMY - SINGLE TROCAR ACCESS. THE TECHNIQUE.

JAMES SKINOVSKY

MARCUS VINÍCIUS DANTAS DE CAMPOS MARTINS

MAURICIO CHIBATA

FERNANDA KEIKO TSUMANUMA

FRANCISCO EMANUEL DE ALMEIDA

INTRODUCTION

The gold standard for treating gallstones is videosurgery for more than 20 years. New surgical approaches have been proposed as substitutes or complementary to the traditional videolaparoscopy, now said conventional, such as NOTES (Natural Orifice Translumenal Endoscopic Surgery), Minilaparoscopy and LESS.Several platforms for the realization of this last approach were developed around the world[1], one of the first to be commercially available was the SITRACC - Single Trocar Access (Edlo, Brazil)[2,3,4]. This chapter focuses on the technique of cholecystectomy performed by this method.

TECHNIQUE

SITRACC platform (Figure 1) consists of a multichannel trocar, with three entries of 5 mm and one with 10 mm, which can be transformed into 5 mm through an own reducer. Curved, articulated end and/or flexible instrumental has been specially created for this approach (Figures 2, 3 and 4). The use of optics of 5 mm, with minimum angle of 30 ° it is highly recommended.

Figure 1 - SITRACC Multichannel Platform

Figures 2 and 3 - Articulated distal extremity - prehension forceps and hook for coagulation

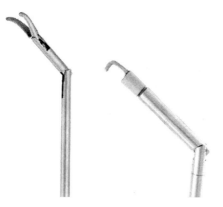

Figure 4 – Disposition of internal and external SITRACC platform and its curved/articulated instrumental

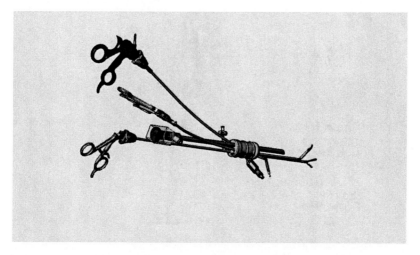

The team position is similar to conventional videolaparoscopic cholecystectomy, but the surgeon must stay more caudally in relation to the

115

patient, on his the left side, as well as the camera (Figure 5).

The multichannel trocar is introduced by Hasson technique through the umbilical scar. It must be noted that better aesthetic results can be obtained through a completely perpendicular intra-umbilical incision, in a way that the future scar is completely hidden within inside natural scar.

After the introduction of the platform, the distal fixator balloon, which has dual function (fixation in the abdominal wall and prevent the reflux of pneumoperitoneum into the exterior), must be inflated with approximately 15 mL of air, externally controlled by the tension of the external marker (Figures 6 a and b). The portals of entry of the platform must remain in the form of a cross, with the entrance orifice largest in the lower quadrant.

Figure 5 - Positioning the surgical team

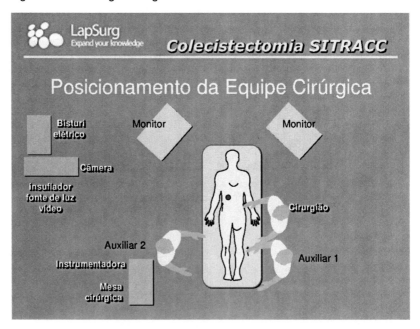

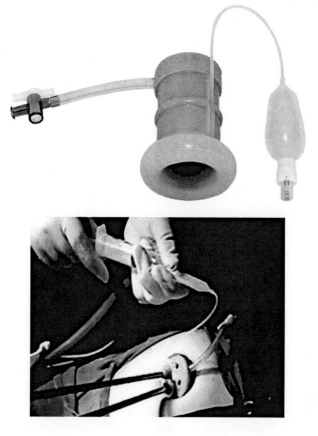

It initially introduced the background totally flexible grasper, which must grasp the vesicular bottom, pulling it toward the diaphragm and at the same time, retracting the liver and facilitating the exposure of the Callot Triangle (Figure 7).

Then the curved prehension forceps (which remains in the left hand of the surgeon) at the left entrance of the platform. This instrument must grasp the gallbladder infundibulum and, with lateral and anterior traction, it must expose adequately the area of Callot, so that the cystic duct and artery are properly visualized.

Next, the instruments for dissection / section are introduced under direct visualization, through the right entrance. These instruments may vary according to the operative moment and its particular strategy, they are: articulated hook (hook) of coagulation, the dissector articulated forceps and curved scissors. It is noteworthy that, at certain times of the surgery, may require the use of conventional laparoscopic rigid instruments, in a hybrid way, especially in cases of advanced inflammatory stage and/or adherence, because they have greater strength of dissection.

The elements of the pedicle are then dissected and isolated, movement facilitated by the distal articulation of the dissector instrumental (Figure 8). These ones are then doubly clipped, using a clipper of 5 mm. In the case of the cystic duct is wide, you can use a 10mm clipper applier (clip LT400) through the south entrance. In this case, the reducer is removed and the 5 mm optics is placed laterally. The curvature of scissors helps greatly in the section(Figure 9).

Following, the gallbladder is dissected from its bed liver, using the coagulation hook with distal articulation (Figure 10). This device allows this action with adequate and ample movements. After dissection of the gallbladder, hemostasis is reviewed and the organ is removed by the interior of the platform, together with the gallbladder, after the distal balloon is deflated (Figure 11).

Figure 7 – Totally flexible grasper - note their dual function - pull the gallbladder and liver retraction

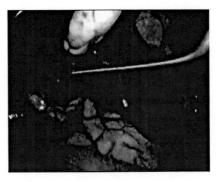

Figure 8 – Isolation of the cystic duct by forceps for articulated dissection

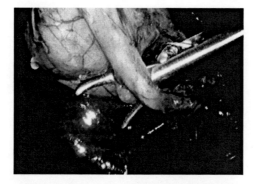

Figure 9 – Section of the clipped cystic duct

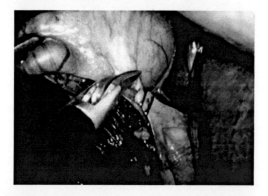

Figure 10 – Dissection of the gallbladder by the articulated hook

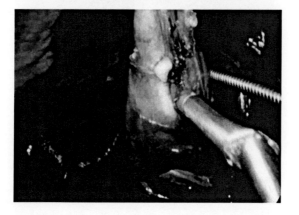

Figure 11 – Removal of the gallbladder inside the platform, posteriorly the balloon is deflated

In difficult cases, it's possible make use of a trocar of 5 mm or even 2 mm, positioned in the right hypochondrium, in order to facilitate the exposition, through the traction of vesicular bottom. When necessary, Penrose drain can be inserted through the platform and removed by the same trocar.

The final scar measures about 20 mm (Figure 12).

Figure 12 – Immediate postoperative results

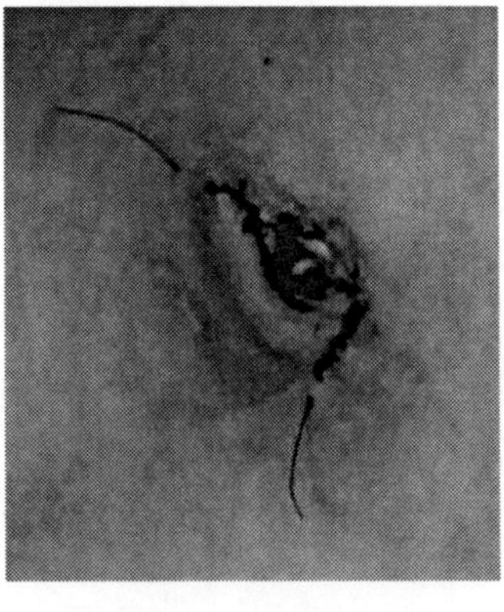

COMMENTS

Due to the difficulty of the own method, the learning demands own learning curve and the team that proposes to perform the method must first attend preparatory courses and simulator training, because the surgeon expert in the conventional laparoscopic approach will certainly find initial difficulties with the peculiarities of the method, as the visualization is not always centered on the monitor, more limited movements, the position of the team and the proper particular manipulation of instruments. In this approach, a cohesive team that works as much time as possible together is crucial for achieving success.

The arrival of new tools and new and longer optics and with the output light source cable at 180^0 will certainly determine make easier the implementation and the consequent greater popularization of this promising surgical method. We should remember that the approach by LESS is part of the Minimal Access Surgery, and, in the event of need, nothing prevents it to become hybrid as required, with elements of minilaparoscopy to assist and, in the near future, even with the aid of a NOTES approach, with the ultimate goal of performing a safe procedure, quick recovery and aesthetic results more satisfactory.

REFERENCES

1. Galvão Neto M, Ramos A, Campos J. Single port laparoscopy Access surgery. Tech Gastrointest Endosc 2009;11(2):84-94.

2. Dantas MVDC, Skinovsky J, Coelho DE, Torres MF. SITRACC – Single Trocar Access: a new device for a new surgical approach. Bras J Vide-Surg 2008; 1(2):60-63.

3. Dantas MVDC, Skinovsky J, Coelho DE. Colecistectomia videolaparoscópica por trocarte único (SITRACC): Uma nova opção. Rev Col Bras Surg 2009; 36(2):177-179.

4. Martins MVD, Skinovsky J, Coelho DE, Ramos A, Galvão Neto MP, Rodrigues J, de Carli L, Cavazolla, LT, Campos J, Thuller F, Brunetti A. Cholecystectomy by single trocar access – SITRACC: The first multicenter study. Surg Innov 2009;Dez – on line - sri.sagepub.com.

SINGLE-ACCESS TRANSUMBILICAL LAPAROSCOPIC CHOLECYSTECTOMY WITH CURVED REUSABLE INSTRUMENTS

Giovanni Dapri

INTRODUCTION

Laparoscopic cholecystectomy is actually considered as the gold standard. Recently, thanks to the advent of the Natural Orifices Transluminal Endoscopic Surgery (NOTES), the attempt to reduce abdominal trauma gained a lot of interest and this procedure became possible to be performed through natural orifices like vagina[1]. The umbilicus can be considered as a natural scar, hence the new trend of single-access laparoscopic surgery and transumbilical cholecystectomy. The technique to perform single-access transumbilical laparoscopic cholecystectomy (SATLC) using curved reusable instruments is described here. Only reusable material is used, hence the cost of the procedure remains similar to standard laparoscopy.

TECHNIQUE

The patient is positioned supine with the arms alongside the body and the legs abducted. The surgeon stands between the patient's legs with the camera assistant to the patient's left (Fig.1). The umbilicus is incised and the peritoneal cavity is entered through the Hasson technique. A purse-string suture using 1 polydiaxone (PDS) is placed in the umbilical fascia at 2, 4, 6, 8, 10, and 12 o'clock positions, respectively. A reusable 11-mm trocar is inserted and a 10-mm, 30°-angled, rigid, standard-length scope is used (Karl Storz Endoskope, Tuttlingen, Germany). Curved reusable instruments (Karl Storz Endoskope, Tuttlingen, Germany) are inserted in the abdomen through the umbilicus without trocars. The curved grasping forceps II (Fig.2a) is inserted through a separate opening, outside the purse-string suture at 10 o'clock through the umbilical fascia. Other instruments as curved coagulating hook (Fig.2b), curved scissors (Fig.2c), curved bipolar scissors (Fig.2d), curved dissecting forceps (Fig.2e), curved suction device and 5-mm straight clip applier (Weck Hem-o-lok, Teleflex

Medical, Belgium) are introduced alongside the 11-mm trocar and inside the purse-string suture (Fig.3). The suture is adjusted to maintain a tight seal around the 5-mm tools and the 11-mm trocar, and opened only permitting the changement of the instruments and the evacuation of the smoke created during dissection. The gallbladder is exposed using the curved grasper. Because of the curved shape of the instruments, the scope never appears in conflict with the instruments' tips (Fig.4a), and the collision of the surgeon's and assistant's hands is avoided (Fig.4b). Variable traction on the gallbladder permits the exposure of the Calot's triangle. As per standard practice, the cystic artery is coagulated or sectioned between the clips, and the cystic duct cutted between clips. The gallbladder is freed from the liver (Fig.5) and removed transumbilically in a plastic bag. The instruments are removed under control, and absorbable sutures are used to close the umbilical fascia and the separate opening used for the grasper. The final scar length is approximately 16 mm (Fig.6).

Fig.1 Patient and team position

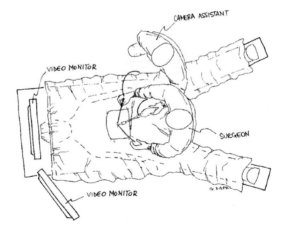

125

Fig.2 Curved reusable instruments according to DAPRI (courtesy of Karl Storz - Endoskope, Tuttlingen, Germany): grasping forceps II (a), coagulating hook (b), scissors (c), bipolar sicssors (d), dissecting forceps (e)

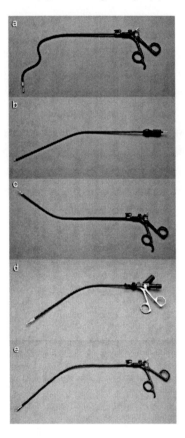

Fig.3 Placement of the curved instruments, scope, and purse-string suture through the umbilicus

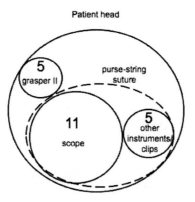

Fig.4 Absence of conflict between the instruments' tips inside the abdomen (a), and between the surgeon's hands outside the abdomen (b)

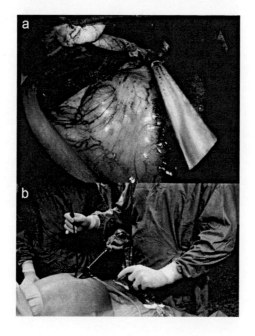

Fig.5 Dissection of the gallbladder from the hepatic bed

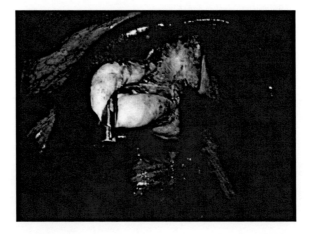

Fig.6 Final scar length

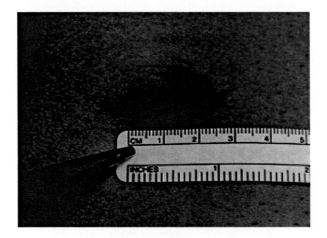

DISCUSSION

The technique of SATLC described here permits surgeons to perform this procedure in similar ergonomic conditions to standard laparoscopy. Thanks to the shaft's curves of the straight classic instruments, surgeon is able to maintain one of the rules of laparoscopy which is the optical system as the bisector of the working triangulation created inside the abdomen as well as outside[2] (Fig.7a,b,c). An advantage of this technique is the final incision length, which is similar to classic laparoscopy because only one 11-mm trocar is used and the instruments are inserted without trocars.

Fig.7 The concept of the curved instruments is based on the creation on the straight classic instruments (a) of the triangulation angle, both externally (b), and inside the abdominal cavity (c).

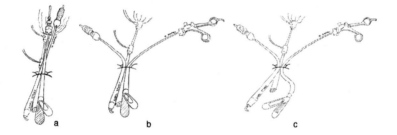

In order to maintain penumoperitoneum during the entire procedure, a purse-string suture is placed in the umbilical fascia. A thick and sliding stitch like 1 PDS is selected. The instrument for the non-dominating surgeon's hand (left), which is the grasping forceps II, is introduced in the umbilical fascia through a separate window, in order to avoid air-leakage at the umbilicus. This instrument remains in the same hand for the entire procedure. The dominating surgeon's hand (right) keeps the other curved instruments, as the coagulating hook, scissors, bipolar scissors, dissecting forceps, suction device and clip applier. Since these instruments are continously changed during SATLC, they're introduced transumbilically just besides the 11-mm trocar and inside the purse-string suture. The purse-string is obviously adjusted to maintain pneumoperitoneum and enlarged permitting the instruments changement and the evacuation of the smoke created with the dissection.

The curved instruments used in the dominating surgeon's hand are similar in shape and present only one curve, created to avoid the collision between the surgeon's and assistant's hands outside the abdomen.

The grasping forceps II has two additional curves besides the main curve at the umbilicus. One curve is created to avoid the conflict with the scope inside the abdomen, and the other one to permit traction of the gallbladder at both infundibulum and fundus. This latter curve is at the opposite position of the classic grasper direction during standard laparoscopy, because it permits to grasp the gallbladder in the different steps of the procedure.

A learning curve to understand in which method the curved instruments have to be maneuvered is obviously necessary, and especially at the beginning of the experience, the curved grasper has to be maneuvered using both hands in order to achieve stability and safety. All the curved instruments have to be inserted transumbilically maintaining a 45° angle in the respect of the abdominal wall.

The selection of the patients for this type of procedure remains fundamental and permits to decrease the conversion rate and the operative time. Patients with acute cholecystitis, gallbladder empyema, body mass index superior to 35 kg/m^2 have to be selected not for SATLC.

Also if a strict selection of patient characteristics is regarded, during SATLC always exists the possibility to place additional trocars to improve the operative field exposure, to treat peroperative complications or to perform peroperative cholangiography[3]. Valid options to increase the Calot triangle's exposure are the placement of percutaneous stitiches[4-6], or millimetrical wire like Veress needle[7], or use of intrabdominal anchors[8-10].

Finally the technique of SATLC described here is performed without use of disposable material, permitting to compare the cost to standard laparoscopy.

REFERENCES

1. Zorron R, Palanivelu C, Galvao Neto MP, et al. International multicenter trial on clinical natural orifice surgery - NOTES IMTN study: preliminary reults of 362 patients. Surg Innov 2010;17:142-58

2. Hanna GB, Drew T, Clinch P, Hunter B, Cuschieri A. Computer-controlled endoscopic performance assessment system. Surg Endosc 1998;12:997-1000.

3. Rao PP, Bhagwat SM, Rane A, Rao PP. The feasibility of single port laparoscopic cholecystectomy: a pilot study of 20 cases. HPB (Oxford) 2008;10:336-40

4. Navarra G, Pozza E, Occhionorelli S, Carcoforo P, Donini I. One-wound laparoscopic cholecystectomy. Br J Surg 1997;84:695.

5. Bresadola F, Pasqualucci A, Donini A, et al. Elective transumbilical compared to standard laparoscopic cholecystectomy. Eur J Surg 1999;165:29-34

6. Rivas H, Varela E, Scott D. Single-incision laparoscopic cholecystectomy: initial evaluation of a large series of patients. Surg Endosc 2010;24:1403-12.

7. Dapri G, Casali L, Dumont H, et al. Single-access transumbilical laparoscopic appendectomy and cholecystectomy using new curved reusable instruments: a pilot feasibility study. Surg Endosc (Epub ahead Aug 31)

8. Elazary R, Khalaileh A, Zamir G, et al. Single-trocar cholecystectomy using a flexible endoscope and articulating laparoscopic instruments: a bridge to NOTES or the final form? Surg Endosc 2009;23:969-72.

9. Dominguez G, Durand L, De Rosa J, Danguise E, Arozamena C, Ferraina PA. Retraction and triangulation with neodymium magnetic forceps for single-port laparoscopic cholecystectomy. Surg Endosc 2009;23:1660-66.

10. Raman JD, Scott DJ, Cadeddu JA. Role of magnetic anchors during laparoendoscopic single site surgery and NOTES. J Endourol 2009;23;781-86.

SINGLE-ACCESS TRANSUMBILICAL LAPAROSCOPIC NISSEN FUNDOPLICATION WITH CURVED REUSABLE INSTRUMENTS

Giovanni Dapri

INTRODUCTION

The procedure of Nissen fundoplication was firstly performed by Rudolf Nissen in 1955 by open access[1]. With the introduction of minimally invasive techniques, Dallemagne et al[2] performed firstly this procedure by laparoscopy in 1991. In 2005 Cadière et al.[3] reported firstly the fundoplication by transoral endoluminal approach.

With the introduction of single-access laparoscopic surgery (SALS), this procedure can be performed by single-incision. The technique of single-access laparoscopic Nissen fundoplication (SALN) performed with curved reusable instruments is described here. The concept of the curved instruments is based on one of the rules of laparoscopy which is the optical system as the bisector of the working triangulation created by the curved instruments inside the abdomen as well as outside[4].

TECHNIQUE

The patient is positioned supine with the arms alongside the body and the legs abducted. The surgeon stands between the patient's legs, the camera assistant to the patient's right, and the scrub nurse to the patient's left (Fig.1). The umbilicus is incised and the peritoneal cavity is entered using the Hasson technique. A purse-string suture using 1 polydiaxone (PDS) is placed in the umbilical fascia at 2, 4, 6, 8, 10, and 12 o'clock positions, respectively. A reusable 11-mm trocar and a 10-mm, 30°-angled, rigid, standard-length scope (Karl Storz Endoskope, Tuttlingen, Germany) are used. Once the pneumoperitoneum is established, curved reusable instruments (Karl Storz Endoskope, Tuttlingen, Germany) are inserted transumbilically without trocars. The curved grasping forceps III (Fig.2a) is inserted through a separate opening, outside the purse-string suture at 10 o'clock through the umbilical fascia. Other instruments as curved coagulating hook (Fig.2b), curved scissors (Fig.2c), curved bipolar scissors (Fig.2d), curved needle holder II (Fig.2e), and curved suction device are introduced alongside the 11-mm trocar and inside the purse-string suture (Fig.3). The suture is adjusted to maintain a tight seal around the 5-mm tools and the 11-mm trocar, and opened only permitting the changement of the instruments and the evacuation of the smoke created during dissection. Thanks to the distal curve of the grasper, the left liver lobe can be retracted contemporary to the exposure of the hepatogastric ligament for the dissection (Fig.4). Both phrenogastric ligaments and crura are freed until to expose the lower esophagus (Fig.5). A piece of umbilical tape, transumbilically introduced, is used to encircle the gastroesophageal junction, increasing the exposure of the hiatus (Fig.6). The umbilical tape is maintained under tension permitting the preparation of both crura for plasty. Silk 2/0 stitches are transumbilically introduced using straight grasper. Cruraplasty is performed by a figure of 8 stitches with intracorporeal knots (Fig.7). The gastric fundus is moved behind the lower esophagus and the short gastric vessels are dissected "à la demand" by medial to lateral approach using the coagulating hook or bipolar scissors (Fig.8). A 34Fr orogastric bougie is pushed down transorally by the anesthesiologist. A floppy 360° fundoplication is performed with intracorporeal knots (Fig.9). Thanks to the curves of the instruments, surgeon works during the entire procedure in ergonomic position with flexed arms (Fig.10). At the end of the procedure, the orogastric bougie, the umbilical tape and instruments are removed under control. Absorbable sutures are used to close the umbilical fascia and the separate opening used for the grasper. The final scar length is less than 2 cm (Fig.11).

Fig.1 Patient and team position

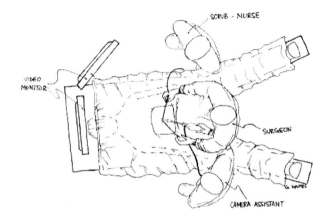

Fig.2 Curved reusable instruments according to DAPRI (courtesy of Karl Storz - Endoskope, Tuttlingen, Germany): grasping forceps III (a), coagulating hook (b), scissors (c), bipolar sicssors (d), needle holder II (e)

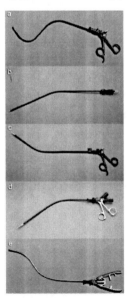

Fig.3 Placement of the curved instruments, scope, and purse-string suture through the umbilicus

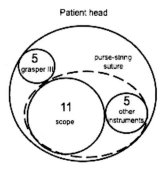

Fig.4 The distal curve of the grasping forceps III permits the retraction of the left liver lobe contemporary to the exposure of the hepatogastric ligament for the dissection

Fig.5 Both crura are freed until to expose the lower esophagus

Fig.6 The lower esophagus is encircled by a piece of umbilical tape

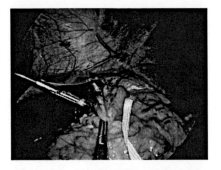

Fig.7 The cruraplasty is performed easily thanks to the jaws opening position on the curved needle holder II

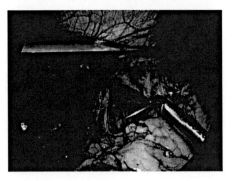

Fig.8 The short gastric vessels are freed "à la demand" after have moved the gastric fundus behind the esophagus (medial to lateral approach).

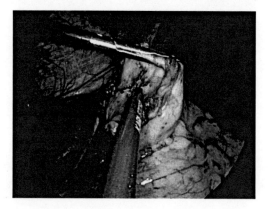

Fig.9 and 10Thanks to the curves of the instruments, a working triangulation is established inside the abdomen (a), and surgeon works during the entire procedure in ergonomic position with flexed arms (b)

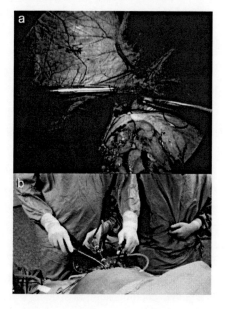

Fig.11 Final scar length

DISCUSSION

In the technique of SALN described here, the curved grasping forceps III is introduced in the abdomen through a separate opening in the umbilical fascia. This is a particular trick to maintain pneumoperitoneum during the entire laparoscopy. The grasper is kept in the non-dominating surgeon's hand (left), and it is never changed during the procedure. Contrary the other curved instruments, kept in the dominating surgeon's hand (right), are changed during the different steps of the procedure. Hence the purse-string suture, placed at the beginning of SALN in the umbilical fascia, helps in maintaining pneumperitoneum and it is opened only for changement of the dominating surgeon's hand instruments or for the evacuation of the smoke created during the dissection. A thick and sliding stitch like 1 PDS is used for purse-string suture.

The curved grasping forceps III and the curved needle holder II mainly present two curves. One curve is at the umbilicus, avoiding the conflict between the surgeon's hands and the scope outside the abdomen, and another curve is between the umbilicus and the instrument's tips, establishing a working triangulation inside the abdomen. The jaws opening of the curved needle holder II are placed at 45° in the respect of the main shaft. This position permits just a quarter rotation of the surgeon's wrist to pass or to remove the stitch in the tissue, and it avoids the potential damage with the viscera inside the abdomen. Furthermore, the distal curve of the grasper permits to push the left liver lobe anteriorly, hereby increasing the operative field exposure. This latter aspect remains one of the main problems during SALS.[5] Other valid options used to increase the exposure of the hiatus are the placement under the liver of a penrose drain suspended by percutaneous suture[6], or placement of stitches at the crura junction[7] or transhepatic percutaneous stitiche for the left liver lobe[8].

The curved coagulating hook, the curved scissors, and the curved bipolar scissors are similar in shape, and present only one curve created to avoid the collision between the surgeon's and assistant's hands outside the abdomen.

All the curved instruments have to be inserted transumbilically following the curves, maintaining a 45° angle in the respect of the abdominal wall.

Thanks to the curved shape, surgeon is able to work in very ergonomic position, similar to classic laparoscopy, because during the entire procedure there is no clushing of the instruments' tips or crossing of the surgeon's hands, as frequently during SALS.[5] Obviously, a learning curve is necessary to understand in which method the curved instruments have to be maneuvered, overall when some sutures have to be performed. Hence, the selection of the patients undergoing to SALN remains an important challenge[9-11], excluding whose presenting body mass index superior to 35 kg/m^2 and giant hiatal hernia. Otherwise the transumbilical approach becomes quite impossibile and the operative time longer.

Finally the umbilical scar length remains similar to the scar used in classic laparoscopy for a 12-mm trocar because only one reusable 11-mm trocar is inserted in the umbilicus and the curved instruments are advanced in the abdomen without trocars. This aspect, added to the fact that all the material is reusable, maintained the cost of SALN similar to the cost of classic laparoscopy.

REFERENCES

1. Nissen R. A simple operation for control of reflux esophagitis. Schweiz Med Wochenschr 1956;86:590-2.

2. Dallemagne B, Weerts JM, Jehaes C, Markiewicz S, Lombard R. Laparoscopic Nissen fundoplication: preliminary report. Surg Laparosc Endosc 1991;1:138-43.

3. Cadière GB, Rajan A, Rqibate M, et al. Endoluminal fundoplication (ELF) - evolution of EsophyX, a new surgical device for transoral surgery. Minim Invasive Ther Allied Technol 2006;15:348-55.

4. Hanna GB, Drew T, Clinch P, Hunter B, Cuschieri A. Computer-controlled endoscopic performance assessment system. Surg Endosc 1998;12:997-1000.

5. Romanelli JR, Earle DB. Single-port laparoscopic surgery: an overview. Surg Endosc 2009;23:1419-27.

6. Hamzaoglu I, Karahasanoglu T, Aytac E, Karatas A, Baca B. Transumbilical totally laparoscopic single-port Nissen fundoplication: a new method of liver retraction: the Istanbul Technique. J Gastrointest Surg 2010:14:1035-9.

7. Tacchino RM, Greco F, Matera D, Diflumeri G. Single-incision laparoscopic gastric bypass for morbid obesity. Obes Surg 2010;20:1154-60.

8. Huang CK, Houng JY, Chiang CJ, Chen YS, Lee PH. Single incision transumbilical laparoscopic Roux-en-Y gastric bypass: a first case report. Obes Surg 2009;19:1711-5.

9. Hong TH, You YK, Lee KH. Transumbilical single-port laparoscopic cholecystectomy: scarless cholecystectomy. Surg Endosc 2009;23:1393-7.

10. Teixeira J, McGill K, Binenbaum S, Forrester G. Laparoscopic single-site surgery for placament of an adjustable gastric band: initial experience. Surg Endosc 2009;23:1409-14.

11. Gill IS, Advincula AP, Aron M, et al. Consensus statement of the consortium for laparoendoscopic single-site surgery. Surg Endosc 2010;24:762-8.

SINGLE-ACCESS TRANSUMBILICAL LAPAROSCOPIC APPENDECTOMY WITH CURVED REUSABLE INSTRUMENTS

Giovanni Dapri

INTRODUCTION

Appendectomy is commonly performed by open surgery through a McBurney incision in the right iliac fossa. Surgeons performing laparoscopy propose minimally invasive technique also to patients presenting acute appendicitis, especially in female patients because gynaecologic pathologies, preoperatively misdiagnosed, can be treated contemporary. Recently, thanks to the new trend of single-incision laparoscopy this procedure can be performed through a single-access. The technique of single-access transumbilical laparoscopic appendectomy (SATLA) is described here, and it is basically founded on one of the rules of laparoscopy which is the optical system as the bisector of the working triangulation created by the curved instruments inside the abdomen as well as outside[1].

TECHNIQUE

The patient is positioned supine with the arms alongside the body and the legs straight. Surgeon stands to the patient's left with the camera assistant to the surgeon's right (Fig.1). The umbilicus is incised and through the Hasson technique the peritoneal cavity is entered. A purse-string suture using 1 polydiaxone (PDS) is placed in the umbilical fascia at 2, 4, 6, 8, 10, and 12 o'clock positions, respectively. A reusable 11-mm trocar is used for a 10-mm, 30°-angled, rigid, standard-length scope (Karl Storz Endoskope, Tuttlingen, Germany). Curved reusable instruments (Karl Storz Endoskope, Tuttlingen, Germany) are inserted in the abdomen through the umbilicus without trocars. The curved grasping forceps I (Fig.2a) is advanced through a separate opening, outside the purse-string suture at 8 o'clock through the umbilical fascia. Other instruments as curved coagulating hook (Fig.2b), curved scissors (Fig.2c), curved bipolar scissors (Fig.2d), curved suction device, and 5-mm straight endoloop device (Ethicon, Johnson & Johnson, Cincinnati, OH) are introduced alongside the 11-mm trocar and inside the purse-string suture (Fig.3). The purse-string is adjusted to maintain a tight seal around the 5-mm tools and the 11-mm trocar, and opened only permitting the changement of the instruments and the evacuation of the smoke created during dissection. The abdominal cavity is checked for the presence of free fluids, and if found a bacteriological sample is obtained. The appendix is exposed using the curved grasper I, and the mesentery is controlled by the curved coagulating hook or bipolar scissors (Fig.4a). Thanks to the curves of the instruments no conflict between the surgeon's and assistant's hands is evidenced (Fig.4b). Preformed knots (endoloops) are placed at the base of the appendix (Fig.5), before its section. A plastic bag, introduced through the 11-mm trocar, is used to remove the appendix transumbilically (Fig.6). The cavity is cleaned and the instruments are removed under control. The umbilical fascia and the separate fascial opening used for the grasper are closed using absorbable sutures. The final scar length is less than 16 mm (Fig.7).

Fig.1 Patient and team position

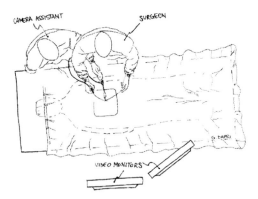

Fig.2 Curved reusable instruments according to DAPRI (courtesy of Karl Storz - Endoskope, Tuttlingen, Germany): grasping forceps I (a), coagulating hook (b), scissors (c), bipolar sicssors (d)

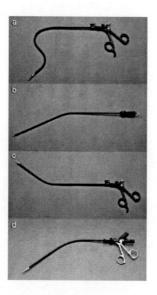

Fig.3 Placement of the curved instruments, scope, and purse-string suture through the umbilicus

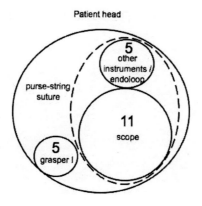

Fig.4 Absence of the conflict between the instruments' tips inside the abdomen (a), and between the surgeon's hands outside (b)

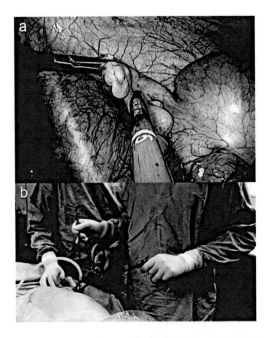

Fig.5 Placement of a preformed knot at the base of the appendix

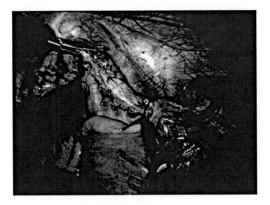

148

Fig.6 Placement of the appendix in a plastic bag

DISCUSSION

Patients with acute appendicitis can be submitted to SATLA but previous properly selection. Diffuse peritonitis, periappendicular abscess, pregnant females have to be considered as exclusion criteria. Peroperative status of the appendix can be more than inflammatory, and in case of perforation, placement of supplementary trocar is mandatory for suturing [2-3], or conversion to classic laparoscopy remains possible[4]. Furthermore the incision used for the potential second trocar is useful for placement of a drainage at the end of the procedure[2].

The curved grasping forceps I is kept during the entire procedure in the dominating surgeon's hand (left) and has two curves. The first curve is at the level of the umbilicus and permits to avoid the conflict between the grasper's handle and the assistant hand. The second curve is inside the abdomen and allows to reach a working triangulation with the other curved instruments. This latter curve has been thought also to obtain bacteriological sample. In case of free fluid in the Douglas pouch, a sample is obtained using curved suction device and retraction of the rectum by the distal curve of the grasper. Obviously a learning curve is needed to move the curved grasper I, and especially at the beginning of the experience both surgeon's hands are necessary to maneuver the grasper with stability and safety.

The other curved instruments as coagulating hook, scissors, bipolar scissors, suction device, and endoloop device are maintained in the dominating surgeon's hand (right). They're similar in shape and present only one curve, created to avoid the collision between the surgeon's and assistant's hands outside the abdomen. Thanks to the curves, surgeon works during the entire procedure in nice ergonomy as standard laparoscopy without clushing of the instruments' tips or crossing of the surgeon's hands.

All the curved instruments are introduced in the abdomen following the curves and maintaining a 45° angle in the respect of the abdominal wall. The curved grasping forceps I is introduced outside the purse-string suture using a separate opening of the umbilical fascia because it is never changed during SATLA. The other curved instruments (for the dominating surgeon's hand), are introduced inside the purse-string suture and alongside the 11-mm trocar. Hence the purse-string suture permits changement of the instruments if enlarged, and maintainance of pneumoperitoneum if tied. Moreover this suture permits the evacuation of the smoke created during the dissection. The stitch selected is 1 PDS, which is thick and sliding to accomodate each instrument changement.

Thanks to the use of a standard trocar and instruments inserted transumbilically witout trocars, the incision length is maintained similar to the scar used during classic laparoscopy for a 12-mm trocar.

Since any disposable material is not used, but only one standard reusable trocar and curved reusable instruments, the cost of the procedure is not increased and remains similar to classic laparoscopy.

REFERENCES

1. Hanna GB, Drew T, Clinch P, Hunter B, Cuschieri A. Computer-controlled endoscopic performance assessment system. Surg Endosc 1998;12:997-1000.

2. Hong TH, Kim HL, Lee YS, et al. Transumbilical single-port laparoscopic appendectomy (TUSPLA): scarless intracorporeal appendectomy. J Laparoendosc Adv Surg Tech A 2009;19:75-8.

3. Dapri G, Casali L, Dumont H, et al. Single-access transumbilical laparoscopic appendectomy and cholecystectomy using new curved reusable instruments: a pilot feasibility study. Surg Endosc (Epub ahead Aug 31).

4. Chouillard E, Dache A, Torcivia A, Helmy N, Ruseykin I, Gumbd A. Single-incision laparoscopic appendectomy for acute appendicitis: a preliminary experience. Surg Endosc 2010;24:1861-5.

SINGLE PORT SURGERY AND BARIATRIC PROCEDURES - CURRENT PERSPECTIVES

Manoel Galvao Neto

Almino Ramos

Josemberg Marins Campos

The use of surgical techniques for the treatment of obesity is constantly evolving. Each publication of specialized magazine or book on the subject, it is notable a large number of studies that seek to improve well-established surgical modalities or even create new tools or techniques that can bring benefits to the patients. This way it was possible to advance from laborious laparotomies, with great damage to the abdominal wall at the beginning of bariatric surgery, to the minimally invasive access of laparoscopy, (FIG 1) which now accounts for the vast majority of bariatric procedures around the world.[1]

Figure 1 – Over the past decades, the trend of modern surgery is to decrease the invasiveness, initially with the transition from laparotomy to laparoscopy and currently to reduce the number of trocars.

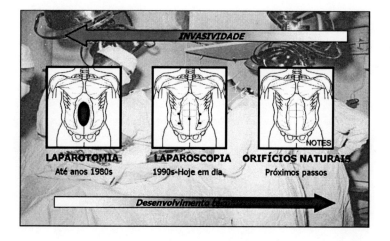

In recent years, a new trend is increasingly being studied in the field of videosurgery, which is the access to the abdominal cavity through a single incision, usually in the umbilical scar. This single access brings in its conception the idea of even less damaging to the abdominal wall, bringing obvious cosmetic benefit and potentially less postoperative pain.[2]

Likewise to the early days of laparoscopy, cholecystectomy is one of the most studied procedures with this new access. [3]However, techniques of bariatric surgery are also being targeted by several studies to use the single incision in its realization. Let's analyze the current state and prospects for the three most common procedures in clinical practice: The adjustable gastric band (AGB), the Sleeve gastrectomy and gastric bypass.

ADJUSTABLE GASTRIC BANDING – AGB

The adjustable gastric band was the first bariatric procedure to be performed by laparoscopy and similarly is the most studied anti-obesity procedure to be performed by a single incision.[4] The need to perform a slightly larger incision than the traditional laparoscopic access in order to introduce the band in the abdominal cavity and puts its port in subcutaneous allows to introduced more than a trocar, facilitating the performance of the procedure, even in the absence of devices specifically designed to perform surgery through a single incision. (FIG 2A, 2B , 2C)

Figures 2A, 2B, 2C – Surgery by single incision for adjustable gastric band: the same incision of the trocar is used for the placement of subcutaneous port.

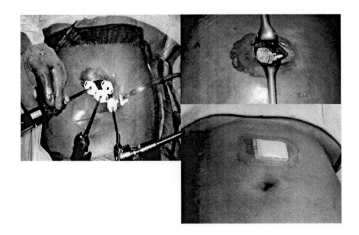

SLEEVE GASTRECTOMY

This new surgical procedure, initially used as part of a major surgery, is gaining more and more space in clinical practice.[1] It is a procedure that involves no anastomosis and that is carried out only in supramesocolic and on a single organ (stomach). Here it is also necessary to perform an incision to remove the surgical specimen, making the use of single incision a good alternative for its performance. (FIG 3) Some authors have already reported these access as safe and effective.[5-8]

Figure 3 – With the use of special trocars, it is possible to introduce at the same time optics, instruments of 5 mm and even a stapler of 12mm to perform Sleeve gastrectomy.

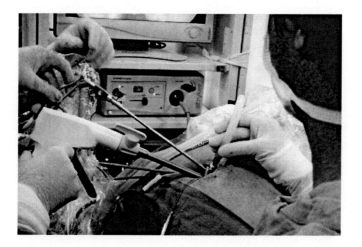

GASTRIC BYPASS

Throughout the world this is the most frequently performed surgery to fight against obesity.[1] Nevertheless, its performance through a single incision at the current time and with the materials available, it seems difficult to use. The difficulty lies in the need to perform intracorporeal sutures and change the (supra and inframesocolic) operative field, which is certainly an obstacle to the use of single incision. However, there are reports in the literature of authors who reduced the number of abdominal trocars and the same report of performance of this technique through a single incision.[9, 10]

FINAL CONSIDERATIONS – PERSPECTIVES

The same way as laparoscopic surgery trailed - and track - a path of validation of results and benefits, we believe that laparoscopy through a single incision should have its value and space in daily clinical practice, acquired through a clear demonstration of benefits achieved with safety and possible use even in centers of medium complexity. This way must initially be performed in centers of teaching and research, with development of specific materials and controlled comparative studies.[11]

REFERENCES

1. Buchwald H, Oien DM. Metabolic/bariatric surgery Worldwide 2008. Obes Surg 2009;19(12):1605-1611.

2. Romanelli JR, Earle DB. Single-port laparoscopic surgery: an overview. Surg Endosc 2009;23(7):1419-1427.

3. Rivas H, Varela E, Scott D. Single-incision laparoscopic cholecystectomy: initial evaluation of a large series of patients. Surg Endosc 2009. Online first.

4. Nguyen NT, Hinojosa MW, Smith BR, Reavis KM. Single laparoscopic incision transabdominal (SLIT) surgery-adjustable gastric banding: a novel minimally invasive surgical approach. Obes Surg 2008;18(12):1628-1631.

5. Saber AA, El-Ghazaly TH. Early experience with SILS port laparoscopic sleeve gastrectomy. Surg Laparosc Endosc Percutan Tech 2009;19(6):428-430.

6. Saber AA, El-Ghazaly TH, Elian A. Single-incision transumbilical laparoscopic sleeve gastrectomy. J Laparoendosc Adv Surg Tech A 2009;19(6):755-758.

7. Arias AF, Prada Ascencio NE, Gomez D, Torres A. Transumbilical Sleeve Gastrectomy. Obes Surg 2009. Online first.

8. Varela JE. Single-site laparoscopic sleeve gastrectomy: preclinical use of a novel multi-access port device. Surg Innov 2009;16(3):207-210.

9. Saber AA, Elgamal MH, El-Ghazaly TH, Elian AR, Dewoolkar AV, Akl AH. Three trocar laparoscopic Roux-en-y gastric bypass: A novel technique en route to the single-incision laparoscopic approach. Int J Surg 2009.

10. Huang CK, Houng JY, Chiang CJ, Chen YS, Lee PH. Single incision transumbilical laparoscopic Roux-en-Y gastric bypass: a first case report. Obes Surg 2009;19(12):1711-1715.

11. Galvao Neto M, Ramos A, Campos J. Single port laparoscopic access surgery. Techniques in Gastrointestinal Endoscopy 2009;11(2):84-93.

MINILAPAROSCOPY - STATE OF THE ART

Gustavo Carvalho

Flávio Augusto Martins Jr

Leandro Totti Cavazolla

INTRODUCTION

The improvement of surgical techniques has led the surgeon to seek means of less invasive access, that cause less trauma and, therefore, cause less pain to the patient, leading to a quicker and less uncomfortable recovery and, if possible, do not leave visible marks of its execution.

With this, came the minilaparoscopy, that can be used in cholecystectomy, appendectomy, in the resection of hepatic and mesenteric cysts, in inguinal herniorrhaphy and in the reflux disease, among others. This approach can also be used in gynecology and thoracoscopy (for sympathectomy, for example) without forgetting the enthusiastic use of minilaparoscopy in pediatric surgery. Minilaparoscopic cholecystectomy is where more frequently the technique is used. The establishment of laparoscopic cholecystectomy as surgery of excellence for the approach of benign gallbladder disease with surgical indication, in the early 90s, it gave enthusiasm to the development of new techniques to bring more benefits to patients.

The idea of miniaturization of the usual instruments from 5 and 10 mm to 2 and 3 mm would be the next stage of laparoscopy as evolution of the surgery, seeking the minimal invasiveness[1,5] (FIGURE 1).

Figure 1 – Instrumental used in Minilaparoscopy

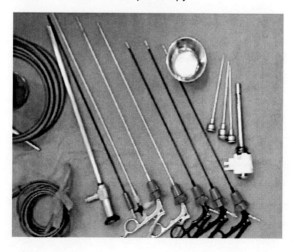

The pioneers of minilaparoscopy with the use of instruments of 2 and 3 mm, at the end of the 90's, stressed its advantages such as less damage to the patient, less pain, quicker recovery, shorter hospitalization time, precocious return to daily activities and better cosmetic effect.

From financial point of view, the miniaturization of the forceps would be an evolution of low cost, because the surgeon would be employing the same principles of laparoscopy with smaller instruments, at a lower cost when compared to other new technologies.

The miniaturization of instruments has raised doubts about its fragility, durability, strength of apprehension, higher cost and degree of difficulty of its use in surgery, if we make parallel with traditional videolaparoscopy, in some cases requiring special training for appropriate use of equipment.

The first publications [11] (Michel Gagner et cols. and Peter Goh et cols.), still with few cases, date back to the late 90's. In the new century came the first randomized studies, comparing minilaparoscopy and traditional laparoscopy. At the moment there is already scientific evidence of great impact to justify the use of this approach, including systematic review of the results of this approach (McCloy[17], 2008). In Brazil, this technique has important defenders (Costa and Silva et cols[7]. and Carvalho et cols [3,4]), with significant and relevant publications on this topic in indexed periodics.

JUSTIFICATION OF MINILAPAROSCOPY

The results found in conventional laparoscopy did conclude that the reduction in the invasiveness of surgical procedures could benefit patients, the extent that there is less tissue damage and, therefore, less metabolic response to trauma. Several studies have tried to analyze the immunological and metabolic changes of laparoscopic surgery. We can cite that, as a consequence to the less trauma would be found, as reported by Novitsky et cols[20] (2004), less amount of inflammatory cytokines, less pain, less changes in the catabolism and less risk of infection. Recently Blinman [2] (2010) published a mathematical model to justify that the summation of several small incisions is not equivalent to a single linear incision when comparing the tension of the incision, which means to say that there is, at least theoretically, an advantage in use the smallest effective trocar. It also reinforced the idea in a letter to the same periodic[6] (2010), through a simple mathematical model that shows the area of trauma of a cylinder with different sizes (figures 2 and 3), noting that the injury caused by a 10 mm trocar is not twice as large as a 5 mm, nor five times greater than a 2 mm, because the lesion or tissue destruction is not only linear, equivalent only to the diameter of the trocar, but the volume of a cylinder, that, is directly proportional to the square of the radius of the trocar for walls of equal thickness.

This manner, the use of minilaparoscopy would reduce in larger proportions the parietal damage and would be used in the attempt to further reduce the stress of surgery.

Figure 2 - Mathematical model that shows the area of trauma of a cylinder with different sizes

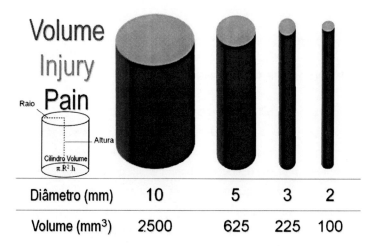

Diâmetro (mm)	10	5	3	2
Volume (mm³)	2500	625	225	100

Figure 3 – Comparative size of the trocars used in conventional videolaparoscopy and minilaparoscopy

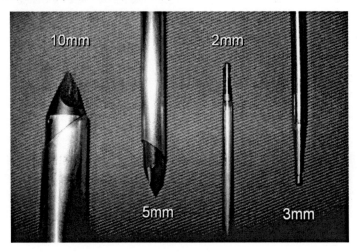

Moreover, since there is a great appeal in today's society for smaller scars, the patients demand for this benefit is supplied, with a considerable attractive cosmetic results of this technique.

MINILAPAROSCOPIC CHOLECYSTECTOMY

DESCRIPTION OF THE TECHNIQUE

Some aspects differ conventional laparoscopic cholecystectomy from minilaparoscopy. The surgical technique is more delicate and accurate, because more flexible and sensitive instruments are used.

The review of the literature about the minilaparoscopy shows great heterogeneity in the application of the technique. It is produced the pneumoperitoneum by the surgeon's preferred technique. The access portals vary from 1.7 mm to 3.5 mm. Most surgeons use a portal from 10 to 12 mm in the umbilical region for the optics and for the use of endoclips. Others, yes,

162

make use of laparoscopic of 5 mm in the umbilical region is also done, but most is 0 °, with poor image quality and considerable fragility and, considering that in most situations it is necessary to remove a surgical piece (which is performed by a portal of 10 mm, most of the time), its use has not justified from technical point of view. The dissection of the gallbladder is made by mono or bipolar electrocautery (dissectors, hooks or a spatula) into the portal of the epigastrium, with instruments of 2 and 3 mm.

In some reports, the cystic duct and arterial duct are clipped using a clipper of 5 or 10 mm, which enters through the umbilical portal, while a 2-3 mm laparoscopic visualize by the epigastrium the ligature with clips of the arterial duct and cystic duct. There are few reports of ligation of the cystic elements with nodes of intracorporeal confection.

The convergence point is the removal of the gallbladder which is always done by the portal of 10 mm through the umbilical scar, introducing the gallbladder in a plastic bag. A variant technique developed and used by our group and endorsed by a expressive casuistry published in the international literature has some significant changes to not use optics minilaparoscopy, which generates important cost reduction and possibility of application in almost any surgical environment which has basic instruments of laparoscopy.

The positioning of staff and portals is illustrated in Figure 4, as well as operation steps in Figures 5, 6 and 7.

Figure 4 – Localization of the team and punches for performing minilaparoscopic

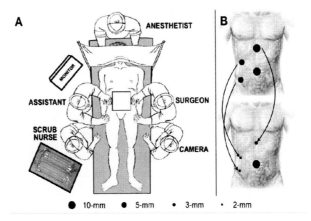

Figures 5, 6 and 7 - Surgical steps of the minilaparoscopic cholecystectomy

5 – Dissection of the gallbladder infundibulum

6 – Ligation of the elements of the vesicular infundibulum

7 – Removal of the gallbladder

The pneumoperitoneum is created by the open technique in the umbilical scar, through a longitudinal incision intra-umbilical, where is inserted a trocar of 10-11 mm with a romba extremity. The patient is submitted to pneumoperitoneum with intra-abdominal pressure ranging from 8-12 mmHg. It is introduced 10 mm optics with 30 ° angle, and under direct visualization is performed three punctures with needle trocar (without valve and without rubber seal), in the abdominal wall. A 3 mm trocar in the epigastrium is used for dissection, cutting, coagulation, irrigation and aspiration. Other 2 trocar of 2 mm is inserted into the right subcostal region, the most lateral for presentation of gallbladder by traction of fundic region toward the diaphragm and the most medial to seizure and presentation of Hartmann's pouch.

Importantly, the placement of trocars must be slightly below the costal margin to not generate the leverage effect and damage the forceps.

After the introduction of the trocars, is carried out evaluation of the abdominal cavity before performing the procedure. In the cases potentially complicated, converts to conventional laparoscopy through the use of 5 mm trocar. The procedure begins with dissection of the infundibulum, the cystic artery is identified and carefully cauterized at approximately 3-5 mm of its length, using monopolar electrocautery near the infundibulum of the gallbladder, avoiding the possibility of accidentally injuring the bile ducts .

The cystic duct is connected with intracorporeal surgical nodes, using wire braided of polyester or polyglactin 2-0 and the hepatic dissection and hemostasis is performed with the monopolar hook electrode.

When necessary, transoperative cholangiography is performed, introducing a needle trocar of 2 mm extra in subcostal region and, through it, a 4F catheter is introduced into the cystic duct.

A bag made with sterile glove fist introduced by umbilical portal, is strategically used to remove the gallbladder, replacing the manufactured collector bags. This bag is essential to avoid the use of optical of 3 mm and provide a safe removal of the gallbladder. After inserting the bag through the portal optics, optics are re-introduced, the gallbladder is placed into the bag and conducted by the forceps more lateral direct to the inside of the optics trocar, under direct vision, where the set is removed. The advantage of clipless technique (Carvalho et col[3,4], 2010), is the possibility of using the minilaparoscopy with a much lower cost, because they avoid the use of endoclips, miniaturized optics and bags manufactured for the extraction of the gallbladder, which certainly increases the cost of the minilaparoscopic method, preventing its further spread[8,9].

The use of surgical nodes of intracorporeal confection, made safely, have shown lower rates of complications with the use of clips. Training in the black box can provide greater training, allowing approaching the time of the ligature with nodes to the use of the clip. All studies, whether series of case, prospective randomized trials or meta-analysis, shows that the minilaparoscopy present longer surgical time, compared to conventional laparoscopy. One of the times of minilaparoscopy which increases the total time of surgery, due to its miniaturization, is the ligature by clips of the cystic duct .

The unavailability of clippers of 2 and 3 mm meant that, some groups used as an alternative the exchange, during surgery, of optics of 10 mm in the umbilical portal by optics of 2 and 3mm, or even 5 mm repositioned the epigastrium portal. In the umbilical portal, then, would pass the instruments of 5 mm or 10 mm to the cystic duct clipping, this adaptation prolongs the operative time. The intracorporeal confection of surgical nodes by well-trained laparoscopists will not increase much more surgical time, because the whole process is performed without the necessity of exchange of optics and with no alteration of image that existed until this beginning of procedures for clipping the cystic duct. The monopolar cauterization through coagulation with current *blend* type in the point the most distal possible to the cystic artery and near the infundibulum of the gallbladder, makes this procedure very secure, since they observe the needed basic care of any videoendoscopic procedure, such as: correct identification of structures and no use of metal clips when you want to use cautery close to them, because they can lead energy and so cause damage to surrounding structures and other cares. The removal of the gallbladder must always be protected through the bag grip glove replacing the collector bags manufactured, allows safe extraction of the gallbladder by a 10 mm trocar without the need of visualization by another trocar to check the perforation of the gallbladder with possible leakage of calculations and bile into the cavity. It also allows the expansion of umbilical aponeurotic incision with minimal aesthetic compromise, in situations of large calculations of the gallbladder.

The procedure is concluded with the closure of the aponeurosis of the access of the umbilical scar and curative without suture of others access of 2 and 3 mm. In a recent publication (Carvalho and cols[4], 2009), was studied the first 1000 cases and the results found were: the average surgical time was 43 minutes (25-127 min). There was no conversion to open surgery. In 2.8% of patients required conversion to conventional laparoscopic cholecystectomy (5 mm). There was no need for conversion to laparotomic surgery in any patient.

Major complications included infection of the umbilical incision (2.1%) and umbilical incisional hernias (1.1%). It was necessary to perform a laparoscopic reintervention for suturing an accessory duct of Luschka type that caused leakage of bile. In this casuistry there were no deaths, damage to the intestines or to the main bile ducts. There was no hemorrhages and no patient required reoperation for open surgery. Postoperatively, patients experienced little pain and great satisfaction with aesthetic results of surgery (Figure-8). The average hospital stay was 16 hours, and 96% of patients were discharged within 24 hours. (Carvalho et cols[3,4]., 2008).

Figure 8 – Aesthetic results of videolaparoscopic cholecystectomy in the 21st postoperative

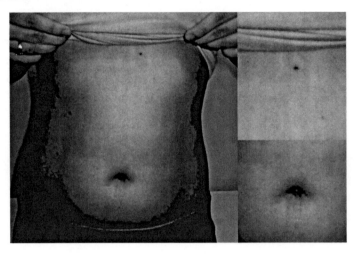

RESULTS OF LITERATURE

However, Hosono et cols[11]. (2007) and McCloy et cols[17]. (2008) criticize the results of the studies used for the manufacture of a meta-analysis, because the methodological quality of some trials made its analysis difficult and decreased their statistical power. Besides the heterogeneity between the techniques and the measures of results, the sample of randomized and controlled trials collected and analyzed in the meta-analysis is small, the largest number with less than 150 cases.

However, in 2004, Lee and cols[13] was already publishing a series of 1011 cases of minilaparoscopic cholecystectomy , that uses two 2 mm trocar, a 5 mm and a 10 mm for optics, using a 5 mm clipper for the cystic duct and cystic artery . There was 0.1% conversion to conventional laparoscopy, to control bleeding from cystic artery. In this study, 10 patients had major complications, and 1 with intra-abdominal abscess, 5 with coleperitoneum, 2 with primary biliary lesions, 1 with a injury of the intestine and 1 by haemoperitoneum.

Eleven patients had minor complications such as wound infection, incisional hernia, adynamic ileus and acute urinary retention. These results show that this is a surgery that can be done safely and for which complication rates are equivalent to those of conventional laparoscopy[19,20,21,22].

The minilaparoscopic cholecystectomy is safe, reproducible and efficient and produces a cosmetic result superior to what we now call conventional laparoscopy.

Its routine use is opposed by high rates of conversion to severe acute cholecystitis, where the difficulty gets bigger and an impediment to continuing the procedure. Most studies reported in the literature excludes of principle the most difficult cases, making it impossible to know the real results in all patients with diseases of the gallbladder, especially in more complex cases[12,13,14,16,17,24,25]. Nevertheless, if performed precociously in the evolution of the disease, minilaparoscopic cholecystectomy in acute cholecystitis appears to be safe and has good results, with no differences with traditional laparoscopy, in addition to smaller incisions and minimal complications, which can be seen in the casuistry of Carvalho and collaborators[4] (2009).

MINILAPAROSCOPIC APPENDECTOMY

While laparoscopic appendectomy is gaining ground as standard surgery for the treatment of acute appendicitis, some studies have shown its first results with even less than 100 cases of minilaparoscopic appendectomy [18.27]. The faster recovery, less pain and better aesthetic results are the advantages cited by these studies.

Laparoscopic surgery is gaining ground in early appendicitis and difficult diagnoses , since it avoids the hassle of expanding an oblique incision in cases where the appendix is located in positions outside of McBurney's point, or to perform other diagnosis in localized pain in the right iliac fossa when the exams do not define the diagnosis. In this context, the initial use of minilaparoscopy can be even more beneficial.

TECHNIQUE OF MINILAPAROSCOPIC APPENDECTOMY

Like the cholecystectomy, the trocar of 10 mm is inserted in the umbilical scar by open technique. The following step is the introduction of a 2 mm trocar in suprapubic region and another of 3 mm in right flank (Fig. 9). It may be necessary to introduce an extra 2 mm trocar to aid in the manipulation of the appendix. After reviewing the cavity observing the four quadrants of the abdomen is confirmed the diagnosis.

Proceeds to identify the base of the appendix at the confluence of the taenia in the caecum, which is dissected and ligated by sutures with double ligature with polyglactin 2-0, even before the appendicular artery dissection. Through the use of a monopolar electrode in forceps dissection proceeds to the next step of the surgery, which is the obliteration by coagulation of the appendicular artery. The appendicular stump is sectioned with scissors of 3 mm above the ligature, as being the appendix inside the grip glove bag confectioned as a bag for the removal of the specimen. In surgeries where there are lots of adhesions of the appendix and which blunt dissection cannot undo them safely, always choose to convert to 5 mm and we used the harmonic scalpel scissors, to, more safely release the appendix.

In these cases you can also add an additional 2-3 mm trocar to assist in the manipulation of the appendix and adhesions. Finally, when necessary, we execute with physiological serum irrigation and aspiration of the cavity for cleaning. The procedure is terminated with the closure of the aponeurosis of the access of the umbilical scar and curative without suture of others access of 2 and 3 mm.

Figure 9 – Arrangement of portals in the Minilaparoscopic Appendectomy

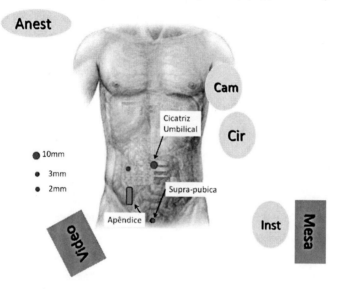

MINILAPAROSCOPIC INGUINAL HERNIA

The first cases of inguinal hernioplasty by minilaparoscopy were published by the end of the last decade by Vara-Thorbeck et cols., Gagner et cols, et Ferzli cols[10,15,23]. The technique used by them was the total extraperitoneal technique (TEPP). Loureiro et cols[10]. (2006) showed the TEPP technique modified with low cost in national specialized periodic, and that its routine use is feasible when evaluating the cost of surgery and postoperative advantages. The performance of TEPP by conventional laparoscopic has a drawback: the operation cost is higher than the hernioplasty by the open

171

technique. However, its modification without the use of the device in balloon to create real space between the peritoneum and the abdominal wall and not even a clipper to fix the mesh in the inguinal region, essential in the conventional videosurgery technique, led to a frequent use of inguinal hernioplasty by videolaparoscopy, with the possibility of natural evolution to minilaparoscopy[26]. After a initial period of adaptation with modified TEPP with conventional forceps, we have selected some cases to minilaparoscopy.

DESCRIPTION OF THE TECHNIQUE

Veres needle is used in the suprapubic region to insufflate gases into the space between the peritoneum and abdominal wall. With the opening in the umbilical scar to the preperitoneal space, we introduce the trocar of 10 mm and we make movements of blunt dissection with optics, in order to separate the peritoneum of the abdominal wall, creating the real pre-peritoneal space.

Once you get space, puncturing the preperitoneal space at the site of Veres needle by direct vision, with trocar of 3 mm and 2 mm more lateral and cephalic in relation to the umbilical scar, in the iliac fossa at the same side to be operated (Figure 10). The structures that were not sectioned by blunt dissection are sectioned with electric scalpel. After dissection and identification of structures of the inguinal region, performs the reduction of the hernia sac. It starts the individualization of the spermatic funiculus, then the accommodation of polypropylene mesh. Next proceeds to the removal of the trocars and deflation of the gas, to the peritoneal space approach, to the abdominal wall without fixing the mesh.

Figure 10 – Arrangement of portals in the Minilaparoscopic Inguinal Hernioplasty

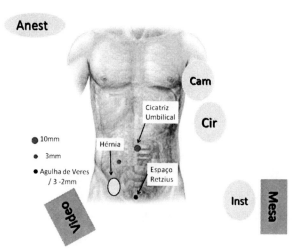

RESULTS

Santoro et cols[23] report good results in their initial series, using glue to fix the mesh and few complications, proving to be a feasible method. Likewise, international publications show security when used trained laparoscopists and the recovery similar to postoperative with the conventional technique. Figure 11 demonstrates the aesthetic result in the immediate postoperative period.

Figure 11 – Aesthetic aspect of the immediate postoperative period of Minilaparoscopic Inguinal Hernioplasty

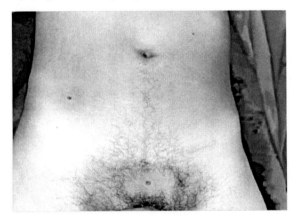

MINITHORACOSCOPIC SYMPATHECTOMY

The sympathectomy by thoracoscopic has revolutionized the treatment of primary hyperhidrosis, because it has less invasibility than the accesses performed previously, before the 90s, allowing the popularization of this approach. The minithoracoscopic technique, which is the only way that we use today, it is performed with an incision of 5 mm to the optics and 3 mm to the optics to the Hook electrocautery (Figure 12).

We perform a surgery each time, for each side. Using double-lumen tracheal probe to ventilate only the contralateral lung, lung deflation occurs as soon as you start the establishment of pneumothorax with low pressures. Punctured cranially above the fourth rib, in the anterior axillary line, by the open technique, using a 5 mm trocar and another above, in the midaxillary line, and one of 3 mm to use of electrocautery.

After sectioning the fibers of the sympathetic chain from T2, T3 and eventually T4 , in selected cases, we pass a Nelaton probe by a 3 mm trocar and began to ventilate the lung again, looking out by the optics its insufflation to

174

almost complete filling of the lung. The positive ventilation continues until the end of the bubble of the serum that we sinks the other end of the Nelaton probe out of the thorax. Despite the image of lower quality and the use of monopolar electrode of smaller diameter, there is no increase in technical difficulty to perform the surgery, there is no considerable increase in the time of its execution, nor compromise of the security in perform it (Figure 13).

The benefit of using smaller trocar with 5 and 3 mm and finest instruments is in lowest risk of injuries of the neurovascular intercostal bundle, especially when the intercostal spaces are narrower, and provide less damage to the thoracic wall, and less pain after surgery.

Figure 12 – Localization of punches to perform Minilaparoscopic Thoracic Sympathectomy

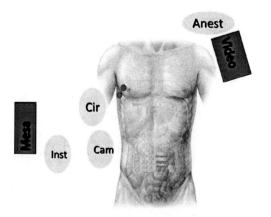

Figure 13 – Intra-thoracic anatomy to perform Sympatectomy

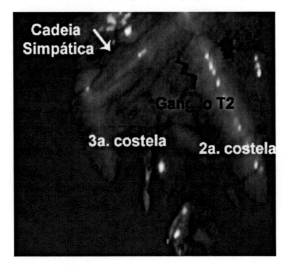

CONCLUSIONS

The minilaparoscopy may be used safely in most of surgery in which laparoscopy operates, providing less damage, less pain, faster recovery and better cosmetic effects. Together with the Surgery by Single Portal and Surgery by Natural Orifice, the Minilaparoscopy has generated excitement and expectation by the lower invasibility. This always leads to questioning what surgical technique will bring the best results with lower risk, performed safely and with costs justifiable to its benefits. We argue that the Minilaparoscopy, as well as other new techniques, will not play this role alone. The future of minimally invasive surgery is the combination of three approaches, because we are combining the advantages and minimizing the disadvantages of each one, potentially resulting in search of the goals of minimal invasibility.

REFERENCES

1.Ahn S, Lee K, Kim S, Cho E, Choi S, Hur Y, Cho Y, Hong K, Shin S, Kim K,Woo Z, Jeong S. Surgical Clips Found at the Hepatic Duct After Laparoscopic Cholecystectomy: A Possible Case of Clip migration. Surg Lap Endosc PercutTech 2005; 15(5):279-282

2. Blinman, T. Incisions do not simply sum. Surg Endosc 2010 jan. epub ahead of print

3.Carvalho G.L., Silva F.W., Cavalcanti C.H., Albuquerque P.P.C., Araújo D.G., Vilaça T.G., Lacerda C.M. Colecistectomia Minilaparoscópicasem Utilização De Endoclipes: Técnica E Resultados Em 719 Casos. Rev Bras Videocir 2007;5(1):5-11

4.Carvalho Gl, Silva Fw, Silva Js, De Albuquerque Pp, Coelho Rde M, Vilaça Tg, Lacerda Cm. Needlescopic Clipless Cholecystectomy As An Efficient, Safe, And Cost-Effective Alternative With Diminutive Scars: The First 1000 Cases. Surg Laparosc Endosc Percutan Tech. 2009 Oct;19(5):368-72.

5. Cavazzola LT. Laparoendoscopic Single Site Surgery (LESS): is it a bridge to Natural Orifice Translumenal Endoscopic Surgery (NOTES) or the final evolution of minimally invasive surgery ? Braz J Videoendosc Surg 2008; 1(3): 93-94.

6.Carvalho Gl; Cavazzola LT. Can mathematic formulas help us with our patients? Surg Endosc, Apr, 2010

7. Franklin Jr. ME, Jaramillo EJ, Glass JL, Trevino JM,Berghoff KF. Needlescopic Cholecystectomy: Lessons Learned in 10 Years of Experience. JSLS 2006; 10: 43–46

8. Golash V. An experience with 1000 consecutive cystic duct ligation in laparoscopic cholecystectomy.Surg Laparosc Endosc Percutan Tech 2008;18(2):155-6.

9. H. Lau, F. Lee A Prospective Comparative Study Of Needlescopic And Conventional Endoscopic Extraperitoneal Inguinal Hernioplasty Surg Endosc (2002) 16: 1737–1740

10.Hosono S, Osaka H Minilaparoscopic Versus Conventional Laparoscopic Cholecystectomy: A Meta-Analysis Of Randomized Controlled Trials. J Laparoendosc Adv Surg Tech A. 2007 Apr;17(2):191-9.

11.Hsieh, C. Early Minilaparoscopic Cholecystectomy In Patients With Acute Cholecystitis, The American Journal Of Surgery 185 (2003) 344

348

12.Lee Pc, Lai Ir, Yu Sc.Minilaparoscopic (Needlescopic) Cholecystectomy: A Study Of 1,011 Cases.Surg Endosc. 2004 Oct;18(10):1480-4. Epub 2004 Aug 24

13.Leggett Pl, Bissell Cd, Churchman-Winn R. Cosmetic Minilaparoscopic Cholecystectomy.Surg Endosc. 2001 Oct;15(10):1229-31.

14.Loureiro Mp. Hernioplastia Endoscópica Extraperitoneal: Custos, Alternativas E Benefícios. Rev Bras Videocir 2006;4(3):135-138.

15. Mamazza J, Schlachta CM, Seshadri PA, Cadeddu MO, Poulin EC. Needlescopic surgery. A logical evolution from conventional laparoscopic surgery. Surg Endosc. 2001 Oct;15(10):1208-12.

16. Mccloy R, Randall D, Schug Sa, Kehlet H, Simanski C, Bonnet F, Camu F, Fischer B, Joshi G, Rawal N, . Is Smaller Necessarily Better? A Systematic Review Comparing The Effects Of Minilaparoscopic And Conventional Laparoscopic Cholecystectomy On Patient Outcomes.Surg Endosc. 2008 Dec;22(12):2541-53. Epub 2008 Sep .

17. Mostafa G, Matthews Bd, Sing Rf, Kercher Kw, Heniford Bt. Mini-Laparoscopic Versus Laparoscopic Approach To Appendectomy. Bmc Surg. 2001;1:4. Epub 2001 Oct 31

18. Novitsky Yw, Kercher Kw, Czerniach Dr, Kaban Gk, Khera S, Gallagher-Dorval Ka, Callery Mp, Litwin De, Kelly Jj.Advantages Of Mini-Laparoscopic Vs Conventional Laparoscopic Cholecystectomy: Results Of A Prospective Randomized Trial.Arch Surg. 2005 Dec;140(12):1178-83.

19. Novitsky YW, Litwin DE, Callery MP. The net immunologic advantage of laparoscopic surgery. Surg Endosc. 2004 Oct;18(10):1411-9

20. Reardon Pr, Kamelgard Ji, Applebaum B, Rossman L, Brunicardi Fc. Feasibility Of Laparoscopic Cholecystectomy With Miniaturized Instrumentation In 50 Consecutive Cases. World J Surg. 1999 Feb;23(2):128-31;

21. Reardon Pr, Kamelgard Ji, Applebaum Ba, Brunicardi Fc. Mini-Laparoscopic Cholecystectomy: Validating A New Approach.J Laparoendosc Adv Surg Tech A. 1999 Jun;9(3):227-32;

22. Santoro E, Agresta F, Buscaglia F, Mulieri G, Mazzarolo G, Bedin N, Mulieri M.Preliminary Experience Using Fibrin Glue For Mesh Fixation In

250 Patients Undergoing Minilaparoscopic Transabdominal Preperitoneal Hernia Repair. J Laparoendosc Adv Surg Tech A. 2007 Feb;17(1):12-5.

23.Sarli L, Costi R, Sansebastiano G. Mini-Laparoscopic Cholecystectomy Vs Laparoscopic Cholecystectomy. Surg Endosc. 2001 Jun;15(6):614-8. Epub 2000 Mar 13.

24.Sarli L, Iusco D, Gobbi S, Porrini C, Ferro M, Roncoroni L. Randomized Clinical Trial Of Laparoscopic Cholecystectomy Performed With Mini-Instruments Br J Surg. 2003 Nov;90(11):1345-8.

25.Skinovsky J., Chibata M., Loureirom.P., Bertinato L.P., Cury A.M., Bonin E.A., Sigwalt M.F. Herniorrafia Inguinal por Videocirurgia pela TécnicaTotalmente Extraperitonial sob Anestesia Locorregional. Rev Bras Videocir 2006;4(4):162-165

26.Wei Pl, Huang Mt, Chen Tc, Weu W, Lee Wj Is Mini-Laparoscopic Appendectomy Feasible For Children. Surg Laparosc Endosc Percutan Tech. 2004 Apr;14(2):61-

ENDOLUMINAL SURGERY – THE PRESENT AND THE FUTURE

Jeffrey Marks

Since the beginning of the 1970s, flexible endoscopy of the gastrointestinal tract has been the dominant modality for the diagnosis of gastrointestinal disease. Over the same period, developments in technology and methodology have made possible the use of endoscopy to treat a host of conditions that once were considered to be manageable only by means of open surgical procedures. The concept of performing endoscopic surgery has become a reality with the advancement of endoscopic therapies to perform mucosal ablation, resection, and tissue approximation. In addition, investigation into intrabdominal therapy has begun with the progression of Natural Orifice Translumenal Endoscopic Surgery.

ENDOSCOPE AND IMAGING TECHNOLOGIES

There have been many recent advances in endoscopic imaging techniques with the goal of improving immediate detection of dysplasia and other mucosal abnormalities. The ability to perform an "optical biopsy" at the time of the endoscopic procedure would enhance directed tissue sampling and resection as well as overall endoscopic therapy. It should be noted that these techniques can be used for both upper and lower endoscopic procedures.

THE PRESENT

CHROMOENDOSCOPY

This technique is based on the staining of mucosal surfaces to differentiate different cellular activities and subtle mucosal abnormalities. Liquids commonly used as topical mucosal agents include Lugol's (potassium iodide) solution, methylene blue, indigo carmine, and Congo red. Diseases including Barrett's esophagus and squamous cell carcinoma of the esophagus have been detected with the use of Lugol's. (1) Normal keratinized squamous epithelium stains a deep brown due to a reaction between the potassium iodide and glycogen, but inflammation, dysplasia, and carcinoma do not stain because of a lack of glycogen. Staining of the esophagus with methylene blue may be useful in the search for Barrett's mucosa: the blue dye is avidly absorbed by the intestinal absorptive cells of the columnar epithelium. (Figure 1) Darkly stained areas may be biopsied for confirmation.

Figure 1. Staining of the esophagus with methylene blue displaying Barrett's mucosa

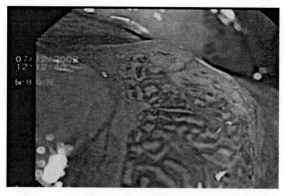

NARROW BAND IMAGING

In narrow band endoscopy, filtered light is used to preferentially enhance the mucosal surface, especially the network of superficial capillaries. (Figure 2) Narrow band imaging is often combined with magnification endoscopy. Both adenomas and carcinomas have a rich network of underlying capillaries and enhance on narrow band imaging, thereby appearing dark brown against a blue green mucosal background. (1)

Figure 2. Narrow band imaging.

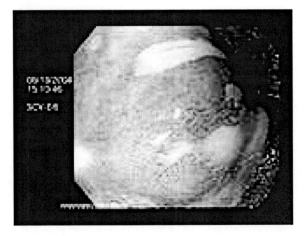

OPTICAL COHERENCE TOMOGRAPHY (OCT)

This technique uses reflection of near-infrared light to produce real-time two-dimensional cross sectional images of the gastrointestinal tract. A small probe similar to an endoscope ultrasound probe which does not require tissue contact is passed through the scope. OCT produces a high resolution image of the layers of the GI tract. (Figure 3) Although not yet in widespread use, investigation into the accurate identification of diseases such as Barrett's esophagus are ongoing. (2)

Figure 3. Optical coherence tomography

DOUBLE-BALLOON ENTEROSCOPY

The double balloon system consists of a dedicated 200 cm endoscope with a balloon mounted distally and a 145 cm overtube with a balloon. The purpose of the overtube is to prevent stretching of the small bowel though which the enteroscope has already traversed. The balloons, whose pressure measures 45 mm Hg when inflated, serve to maintain the position of the scope and overtube. (Figure 4) Clinical studies have documented 88% success of complete examination of the small bowel in total enteroscopy (upper and lower) cases. (3)

Figure 4. Double balloon enteroscope

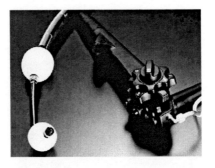

THE FUTURE

AUTOFLUORESCENCE

Autofluorescence endoscopy relies on several principles: tissue architecture changes such as mucosal thickening dampen submucosal autofluorescence; neovascularization alters the light emitting and scattering properties of surrounding tissue; the biochemical microenvironment, such as high oxidation-reduction activity, alters autofluorescence; and different tissue types have unique distribution of fluorophores. Autoflurescence endoscopy has been shown in pilot studies to improve the detection of dysplasia in Barrett's esophagus and chronic ulcerative colitis. (4) (Figure 5)

Figure 5. Autoflourescence imaging

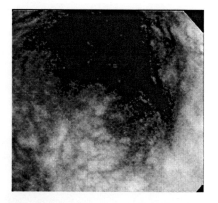

LIGHT SCATTERING SPECTROSCOPY

Light scattering spectroscopy mathematically analyzes the intensity and wavelength of reflected light to estimate the size and degree of crowding of surface epithelial nuclei. The technique relies on absorption and scattering of white light. Small clinical trials using light scattering spectroscopy have shown efficacy in detecting Barrett's esophagus and early colonic dysplasia. The technique relies on graphing mathematical computations rather than an optical biopsy in other emerging imaging techniques. Light scattering spectroscopy might be used in combination with optical biopsy for detection of early dysplasia. (4)

CONFOCAL FLUORESCENCE MICROENDOSCOPY

Standard endoscopy uses white light to visualize a large surface area with relatively low resolution. In contrast, confocal endoscopy aims to visualize the mucosa and submucosa with subcellular resolution, a technique deemed optical biopsy. (Figure 6) The process of confocal magnification reduces out-of-focus light from above and below the focal plane at a magnification of 1000x. The system is designed to measure tissue fluorescence, therefore an exogenous fluorophore (a molecule which causes another molecule to be fluorescent) is usually administered. Varying depths of tissue are examined by altering the focal plane, and images from different depths are stacked together to create an optical slice of tissue, thus the term optical biopsy. (4)

Figure 6. Confocal Fluorescence Microendoscopy

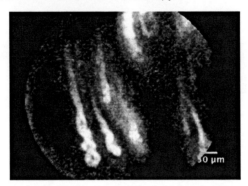

SELF-PROPELLED COLONOSCOPES

In an effort to simplify the process of colonoscopic screening, self-propelled endoscopes are in development. The Aer-O-Scope (GI View, Ltd, Ramat Gan, Israel) is a user-independent, self-propelled, self-navigating colonoscope. (Figure 7) The device consists of a disposable rectal introducer, supply cable, and a scope embedded within a scanning balloon. A small pilot study examined the proof of concept of the Aer-O-Scope. In a cohort of young volunteers (ages 18-43 years), the device successfully reached the cecum in 83% of cases. There were no device-related complications. The device contains no working channel for therapeutic interventions, therefore it is intended for screening purposes only. (5)

Another self-propelled colonoscope, the ColonoSight (Stryker Corp, Kalamazoo, MI) employs air-assisted propulsion in a disposable system. (Figure

188

8) A pneumatic mechanism generates the pressure to create the forward force while an operator directs the scope using handles. The system uses light emitting diode optics, rather than video or fiber optics, and has disposable working channels. A pilot study for ColonoSight reported intubation of the cecum in 88% of cases at a mean time of 12 minutes without any device-related complications. (5)

Figure 7. Aer-o-scope self-propelled endoscope

Figure 8. ColonoSight prototype endoscope

Figure 8

ENDOSCOPIC THERAPEUTIC TECHNIQUES

THE PRESENT

ENDOSCOPIC MUCOSAL RESECTION

Applications for endoscopic banding include treatment of mucosal neoplasia in conjuction with endoscopic mucosal resection (EMR). The treatment of premalignant as well as superficial cancers can now be managed by endoscopic resective techniques. Endoscopic mucosal resection (EMR) has been employed for adenomas, dysplastic lesions, and early-stage carcinomas, including lateral spreading tumors. Multiple technical variations of EMR for the upper and lower tract have been developed, including submucosal injection, "suck-and-cut," "suck-and-ligate," and strip biopsy. (6-8)

SALINE LIFT EMR

The most commonly performed EMR technique employs submucosal injection of a fluid followed by electrosurgical polypectomy. The most commonly used fluid is saline with or without epinephrine, although hyaluronic acid, glycerol, and dextrose have all been described. (9,10) A bleb is created with the submucosal injection creating space between the line of resection and the muscularis propria of the organ, and the lesion is resected. One caveat to this technique is that if the submucosal injection does not result in elevation, one must consider that this mass is an invasive lesion and should not be resected endoscopically.

"SUCK-AND-CUT" EMR

The "suck-and-cut" technique uses a specially designed cap attached to the tip of the endoscope. A submucosal injection may be created initially as with the saline lift EMR, and the lesion is sucked into the cap. A snare affixed inside the cap is used to encircle the lesion and it is then resected by application of electrocautery similar to snare polypectomy. Similar to any thermal technique, risk of perforation exists.

"SUCK-AND-LIGATE" EMR

The "suck-and-ligate" technique transforms a sessile or nodular lesion into an artificial pedunculated polyp, which can then be resected with standard polypectomy techniques. A band ligating device is attached to the tip of the endoscope and the tissue is sucked into the cap and a band is placed at the base of the lesion. This is done with or without saline lift injections prior to banding. The site is then resected with a snare similar to routine snare polypectomy.

The most frequent complications of EMR are bleeding and perforation. Immediate bleeding can be controlled with endoscopically placed clips or injection of dilute epinephrine. Electrocautery should be used judiciously after EMR because the thin submucosa and serosa are susceptible to full-thickness injury with cautery. Delayed bleeding often requires repeat endoscopy with injection therapy or clip application, although angiography and embolization may be an alternative. Perforations can also be managed endoscopically with endsocopic clips as well as temporary enteral stent placement to cover the site of perforation. The rate of perforation after EMR is as high as 5% for large lesions in the right colon. (6)

Endoscopic mucosal resection has been employed for adenomas, dysplastic lesions, and early-stage carcinomas including lateral spreading tumors. (6,11) Carcinomas without submucosal invasion or nodal spread might be amenable to EMR. CT scan and endoscopic ultrasound is recommended to assess for nodal disease prior to EMR. (12,13) Despite clean resection margins from EMR, recurrence rates of early-stage carcinomas might be as high as 40%. (14,15)

ENDOSCOPIC SUBMUCOSAL DISSECTION

An extension of EMR that has been recently reported for endoscopic resection of more extensive lesions is endoscopic submucosal dissection (ESD). Utilizing a combination of needle cautery and blunt endoscope cap dissection, large segments of tissue can be resected. The potential advantage of ESD is that it represents a more classic oncologic procedure as compared to the piece meal resection that occurs with other EMR techniques in that margins as well as lesion depth can be more accurately pathologically evaluated. Complications may be higher for ESD than for the other EMR techniques, including bleeding, perforation, and stricture formation. (16)

ENDOSCOPIC MUCOSAL ABLATION

Endoluminal therapies for ablation of mucosal based diseases such as Barrett's esophagus have recently seen great advances. Endoscopic Radiofrequency Ablation (RFA) is a relatively new technology that has recently gained acceptance for treatment of intestinal metaplasia as seen in Barrett's esophagus. (17) (Figure 9)A balloon based system, as well as a directed planar electrode device implementing this technology, have been used in this form of therapy. Several studies have proven feasibility and safety for this novel therapy, with very few documented cases of post-procedural structuring as had been seen with PDT. (18) Further studies documenting long term effects of this therapy, as well as the absence of buried submucosal metaplastic glands or cancer are still necessary.

Figure 9. Barrx balloo-based endoscopic RFA mucosal ablation

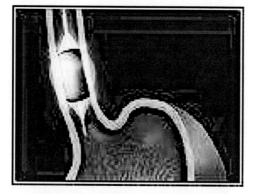

ENDOSCOPIC STENT TECHNOLOGY

Endoscopic stents can be utilized for the treatment of strictures, leaks, fistulae, and obstructing neoplasms. (19-21) The delivery system is dependent on the type of stent and the location for deployment. Endoscopic stent deployment is either through-the-scope (TTS), or wire guided using fluoroscopic guidance. TTS stents are delivered through the endoscope channel and are routinely a 10Fr system and require a therapeutic scope. Non-TTS stents are limited to the esophagus including the esophagogastric junction or the rectosigmoid region. In patients following gastric resection, these systems can also traverse a gastrojejunal anastomosis.

The characteristics of the actual endoscopic stents is quite diverse. There are different lengths, widths, and morphology of stents. In addition, stents can be uncovered, partially covered, or fully covered. Covered endoscopic stents have been created for the sole purpose of temporarily bridging esophagaeal and proximal anastomotic leaks and fistulae. (Figure 10) These stents are considered removable as there is minimal tissue in-growth, which occurs usually at the proximal and distal ends. The greatest problem with these stents is the high risk of migration. (21) Bleeding, perforation, and obstruction are far less common complications.

Figure 10. Fully covered esophageal stent

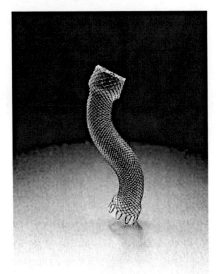

Uncovered enteral stents, utilizing TTS deployment systems, are not intended for removal and can be placed for temporary relief of benign and malignant strictures throughout the gastrointestinal tract. (Figure 11) They are associated with tissue in-growth and occasional occlusion if they are left in place, but they have a lower rate of migration. In unresectable disease states, palliation of obstruction with enteral stents can provide an alternative to surgical bypass procedures. (22-26)

Figure 11. Endoscopic image after deployment of an uncovered enteral stent

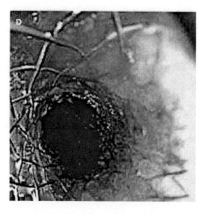

ENDOLUMENAL THERAPY FOR GASTROESOPHAGEAL REFLUX DISEASE

There has been a wide array of endoscopic devices and techniques recently introduced for the management of gastroesophageal reflux. Mucosal suturing devices have shown limited efficacy, and injectable prosthetics have engendered concerns for patient safety. Both a full thickness suturing system and delivery of radiofrequency energy to the esophagogastric junction have been shown to be safe and effective in reducing the symptoms of reflux and possibly providing a barrier to distal esophageal acid exposure. The majority of GERD endoluminal therapies have been abandoned due to lack of efficacy or to economic pressures and resultant industry collapse.

THE FUTURE OF ENDOSCOPIC THERAPIES

The future in endoscopy will be based on advancements of both the tools and the applications available to endoluminal therapy. Intraluminal and translumenal endoscopic techniques are being proposed as potential surgical alternatives, taking on an increasingly more invasive and therapeutic role.

Recent interest in natural orifice translumenal endoscopic surgery (NOTES) united surgeons and gastroenterologists with the desire to access the abdominal cavity via naturally existing orifices including the stomach, colon, bladder, and vagina. An appropriate application for this approach is still yet to be elucidated. It is theorized that NOTES may have distinct advantages over laparoscopy in that it may not necessarily require a sterile working environment to perform, and it possibly could also be completed under conscious sedation similar to other endoscopic procedures. (27, 28)

The obvious limitations to NOTES were based on the lack of adequate and appropriate endoscopic equipment. It was apparent early on that stable platforms would be necessary as well as endoscopic tools for cutting, hemostasis, and tissue manipulation. Transoral and transvaginal multichannel platforms with internal capability for manipulation and fixation are now becoming available. Scissors, suturing devices, bipolar forceps, and grasping devices are a few of the novel instruments soon to be added to the endoscopist's armamentarium. Dual channel endoscopes are currently available and useful for techniques such as strip biopsy. A future scope might allow triangulation of the optical perspective and the instrumentation, as is used in laparoscopy.

These tools, however, will have a more likely impact on other endoscopic therapies including intraluminal endoscopic surgery. The ability to perform full thickness resection, intraluminal anastomoses, and closure of perforations are all likely procedures to be seen in the very near future. The tools created for both intraluminal and translumenal interventions will allow the endoscopist to continue to supplant surgical therapies for numerous gastrointestinal diseases. The integration of flexible endoscopic techniques into the armamentarium of the GI surgeon permits a more multidimensional approach to the treatment of digestive disease. The modern surgeon must continue to stay abreast of these endoscopic advances to provide appropriate patient care.

REFERENCES

1) Chiu HM, Chang CY, Chen CC, Lee YC, Wu MS, Lin JT, Shun CT, Wang HP. A prospective comparative study of narrow-band imaging, chromoendoscopy, and conventional colonoscopy in the diagnosis of colorectal neoplasia. Gut. 2006

2) Isenberg G, Sivak MV Jr, Chak A, Wong RC, Willis JE, Wolf B, Rowland DY, Das A, Rollins A. Accuracy of endoscopic optical coherence tomography in the detection of dysplasia in Barrett's esophagus: a prospective, double-blinded study. Gastrointest Endosc. 2005 Dec;62(6):825-31.

3) Monkemuller K, Weigt J, Treiber G, Kolfenbach S, Kahl S, Rocken C, Ebert M, Fry LC, Malfertheiner P.Diagnostic and therapeutic impact of double-balloon enteroscopy. Endoscopy. 2006 Jan;38(1):67-72.

4) Sivak MV.Gastrointestinal endoscopy: past and future. Gut. 2006 Aug;55(8):1061-4.

5) Ponsky JL.Endoluminal surgery: past, present and future. Surg Endosc. 2006 Apr;20 Suppl 2:S500-2.

6) Conio M, Ponchon T, Blanchi S, Filiberti R. Endoscopic mucosal resection. Am J Gastroenterol Am J Gastroenterol. 2006; 101(3):653-63.

7) .Uraoka T, Saito Y, Matsuda T, et al. Endoscopic indications for endoscopic mucosal resection of laterally spreading tumourtumors in the colorectum. Gut. 2006; 55(11):1592-7.

8) .Beck DE. Advances in gastrointestinal endoscopic techniques. Surg Clin North Am Am Surg. Clin North Am. 2006; 86(4):849-65.

9.Uraoka T, Fujii T, Saito Y, et al. Effectiveness of glycerol as a submucosal injection for EMR. Gastrointest Endosc 2005; 61(6):736-40.

10 .Fujishiro M, Yahagi N, Kashimura K, et al. Comparison of various submucosal injection solutions for maintaining mucosal elevation during endoscopic mucosal resection. Endoscopy. 2004; 36(7):579-83

11.Hurlstone DP, Sanders DS, Cross SS, et al. Colonoscopic resection of lateral spreading tumourtumors: a prospective analysis of endoscopic mucosal resection. Gut. 2004; 53(9):1334-9.

12.Ahmad NA, Kochman ML, Ginsberg GG. Endoscopic ultrasound and endoscopic mucosal resection for rectal cancers and villous adenomas. Hematol Oncol Clin North Am. 2002; 16(4):897-906.

13.Waxman I. EUS and EMR/ESD: is EUS in patients with Barrett's esophagus with high-grade dysplasia or intramucosal adenocarcinoma necessary prior to endoscopic mucosal resection? Endoscopy. 2006; 38 Suppl 1:S2-4.

14.Bories E, Pesenti C, Monges G, et al. Endoscopic mucosal resection for advanced sessile adenoma and earlystage colorectal carcinoma. Endoscopy. 2006; 38(3):231-5.

15.Tamura S, Nakajo K, Yokoyama Y, et al. Evaluation of endoscopic mucosal resection for laterally spreading rectal tumors. Endoscopy. 2004; 36(4):306-12.

16. Chennat J, Konda VJ, Ross AS, et al. Complete Barrett's eradication endoscopic mucosal resection: an effective treatment modality for high-grade dysplasia and intramucosal carcinoma--an American single-center experience. *Am J Gastroenterol.* 2009 Nov;104(11):2684-92.

17. Avilés A, Reymunde A, Santiago N. Balloon-based electrode for the ablation of non-dysplastic Barrett's esophagus: ablation of intestinal metaplasia (AIM II Trial).*Bol Asoc Med P R.* 2006 Oct-Dec;98(4):270-5.

18. Chennat J, Konda VJ, Ross AS, et al. Complete Barrett's eradication endoscopic mucosal resection: an effective treatment modality for high-grade dysplasia and intramucosal carcinoma--an American single-center experience *Am J Gastroenterol.* 2009 Nov;104(11):2684-92.

19. Keränen I, Udd M, Lepistö A, et al. Outcome for self-expandable metal stents in malignant gastroduodenal obstruction: single-center experience with 104 patients. *Surg Endosc.* 2009 Sep 3. [Epub ahead of print].

20. Moon JH, Choi HJ, Ko BM, et al. Combined endoscopic stent-in-stent placement for malignant biliary and duodenal obstruction by using a new duodenal metal stent (with videos). *Gastrointest Endosc.* 2009 Oct;70(4):772-7.

21. Babor R, Talbot M, Tyndal A. Treatment of upper gastrointestinal leaks with a removable, covered, self-expanding metallic stent. *Surg Laparosc Endosc Percutan Tech.* 2009 Feb;19(1):e1-4.

22. .Ely CA, Arregui ME. The use of enteral stents in colonic and gastric outlet obstruction. Surg Endosc Surg Endosc. 2003; 17(1):89-94.

23.Meisner S, Hensler M, Knop FK, et al. Self-expanding metal stents for colonic obstruction: experiences from 104 procedures in a single center. Dis Colon Rectum. 2004; 47(4):444-50.

24.Xinopoulos D, Dimitroulopoulos D, Theodosopoulos T, et al. Stenting or stoma creation for patients with inoperable malignant colonic obstructions? Results of a study and cost-effectiveness analysis. Surg Endosc 2004; 18(3):421-6.

25.Baik SH, Kim NK, Cho HW, et al. Clinical outcomes of metallic stent insertion for obstructive colorectal cancer.Hepatogastroenterol.ogy 2006; 53(68):183-7.

26.Ng KC, Law WL, Lee YM, et al. Self-expanding metallic stent as a bridge to surgery versus emergency resection for obstructing left-sided colorectal cancer: a case-matched study. J Gastrointest Surg J Gastrointest Surg.2006; 10(6):798-803.

27. Onders, R; McGee, MF; Marks, J, et al. Diaphragm Pacing With Natural Orifice Transluminal Endoscopic Surgery (NOTES): Potential For Difficult To Wean Intensive Care Unit (ICU). *Surgical Endoscopy*, 2007, v21 n3, 475-9.

28. Marks, J; Ponsky, J; Pearl, J; et al. PEG "Rescue": A Practical NOTES Technique. *Surgical Endoscopy*, 2007, v21 n5 816-9.

ENDOLUMINAL PROCEDURES: TREATMENT OPTIONS FOR MORBID OBESITY

Sérgio Roll

INTRODUCTION

Bariatric surgery has changed a lot over the last decade. The faster growth and greater interest in this field can be largely attributed to the application of minimally invasive techniques, used in these complex procedures. Low-risk procedures, such as adjustable gastric banding and the evidences that demonstrate the safety and benefits of laparoscopic gastroplasty, had caused a growing acceptance of these procedures between patients and physicians[1].

Currently, more than 220.000 bariatric procedures are performed annually in the United States [2]. These numbers are only 1,6% of the 13.750.000 individuals with morbid obesity in the United States that satisfy the NIH criteria to perform the bariatric surgery. However, there are still many obstacles to the acceptance of these procedures and patients' access to them.

There are many reasons for the low acceptance of bariatric surgery; however, it is safe to say that no technique is ideal, and the current procedures have associated risks[3]. An additional factor to be considered is that, in most cases, the patient's preference determines the type of procedure to be performed.

The emergence of new less invasive technologies, that can be performed endoscopically (with presumably much lower risk), has great potential to attract new patients for the treatment of morbid obesity and try to improve the rates of complications associated with conventional procedures[1].

Another important question for bariatric surgery is the regained of weight after 3 to 5 years of initial surgical procedure[4].

Several devices have been applied in several postoperative problems of Y Roux gastroplasty, as dilation of the neo-stomach, dilation of the gastrojejunal-anastomosis, loss of silicone ring in the case of Capella technique and in cases to repair the fistula, in an attempt to reduce the risks and complications associated with traditional revisional surgery[4-5].

PRIMARY ENDOSCOPIC PROCEDURES:

INTRAGASTRIC BALLOON FOR ENDOLUMINAL RESTRICTION

One of the first devices used was the Garren-Edwards bubble. The initial concept of a cylindrical device, which extends across the space of the stomach endoscopically placed was proposed in 1982. Approved in 1985 by the Food and Drug Administration (FDA) and withdrawn in 1988 due to poor patient tolerance and bad results, and to its efficiency, demonstrated in several placebo-controlled trials[6].

The mechanism of action of the balloon may occur through mechanical satiety, delayed gastric emptying, hormone modulation, neuronal effects, behavior modification, or placebo.

Advantages include ease of placement under sedation, the fact that it is reversible or temporary and low morbidity. Disadvantages include the small weight loss and recovery of this, after balloon withdrawal. There is in the market an improved version of the Garren-Edwards bubble, produced by BioEnterics Intragastric Balloon (BIB) System (Allergan, Irvine, Calif.), which was launched in mid-1990. This system includes a silicone balloon, that is filled with 400 to 700cc of physiological saline. It is also in the stomach of a patient for a maximum period of six months. Although the device is not approved by FDA for use in the U.S., European and Latin American experience is quite extensive. Genco et al[7] reported the Italian experience in a retrospective study of efficacy and reduction of comorbidities. The study included 2.515 patients over four years of follow-up, with body mass index (BMI) of 44,4kg/m^2 and one or more comorbidities in 56,4% of patients. After six months of introduction of balloon, the mean BMI dropped from 44.4 to 35.4kg/m^2, with average loss of overweight of 33.9%. A relevant fact was the improvement in comorbidities in 1,242 of 1,394 (89.1%) patients. Among the complications reported, we find: gastric perforation in five patients (0,19%), 19 with gastric obstruction (0,76%), nine of the balloon ruptures (0,36%), 32 patients with esophagitis (1,27%), five patients with gastric ulcer (0,19%), and 11 balloons removed due to intolerance of the patient (0,44%).

SUTURES AND DEVICES OF STAPLING AND FOR ENDOLUMINAL RESTRICTION

Endoscopic vertical gastroplasty (EVG) was described by using an endoscopic suture device, attached to the tip of the endoscope (Endoscopic Sewing Nachine) (CR Bard Inc., Murray Hill, NJ). This instrument performs endoluminal sutures, fixing a plastic ring in the gastric wall. The procedure is performed with the suture in the small gastric curvature of a plastic ring, from 3 to 8 cm of the esophageal gastric junction. A tube of 8 cm in length is created along the lesser curvature of stomach, suturing the anterior and posterior walls of the stomach with Endoscopic Sewing Machine (ESM). This study was conducted only in the stomachs of pigs explanted[8].

Olympus developed the Eagle Claw Endoscopic Suturing Device (Olympus Corporation, Tokyo, Japan), which performs endoscopic sutures. It was used in a pig model to create a small gastric pouch entirely within the stomach of a pig explanted[9]. This bag is about 100cc. After some studies, the authors admitted that the size of gastric pouch was too large to result in a considerable weight loss in morbidly obese patients[10]. The point was to demonstrate the feasibility of performing a purely endoluminal procedure to decrease the gastric volume. The same group published another set of experiments in four animals, which were kept alive, and this time, the gastric pouch had a capacity of 30cc. The investigation was limited by its design as a study of acute feasibility and short-term success has not been evaluated[11].

The Bard EndoCinch Suturing System (CR Bard, Inc., Murray Hill, New Jersey) is an experimental device for endoluminal vertical gastroplasty (EVG). This device uses a suction capsule and another one that performs the suture at the tip of the endoscopic apparatus.

In 2005, Fogel et al conducted a feasibility study in 10 obese patients with a BMI range between 28 to 43kg/m^2. The procedure was technically successful in all patients, with a mean time of performance between 60 to 90 minutes, without complications, and a weight loss between 15 and 49 kg in nine months of follow-up.

A second study was performed in 2008 by Fogel et al, in a series of 64 patients with a BMI of 28 to 60.2kg/m^2. The mean procedure time was 45 minutes, with no serious adverse events. Patients reported a significant reduction of hunger and amount of food eaten, early satiety. The first results of weight loss were similar to traditional bariatric procedures, with a significant reduction in BMI at 1, 3 and 12 months from performance of the procedure. The patients had a significant percentage of overweight loss (± SD) of 21,1% ± 62%, 39,6% ± 11,3% and 58,1% ± 19,9% at 1, 3 and 12 months of follow up, respectively. Fifty-nine of 64 patients (94,1%) were successfully observed, with 12 months of follow-up. Fourteen endoscopies were performed sometime between 3 and 12 months. Of these 14 endoscopies, five patients had the configuration of the suture intact, six patients had EVG partially intact and three had lost the procedure performed[12].

A new generation of this device (Restore Suturing System ™) is being evaluated by a multicenter study, prospective, nonrandomized, in the United States involving two centers (Brigham and Women's Hospital, Boston, Massachusetts, and Cleveland Clinic, Cleveland, Ohio), with it being designed for two year of follow-up[13].

Another endoluminal clamping device performing a transoral gastroplasty was reported in two recent studies in humans in Belgium and Mexico. The system of transoral gastroplasty (TOGA ™) (Satiety Inc., Palo Alto, Calif.) was used to create a transmural stapling, performing a restrictive pouch along the lower curvature of the stomach. This study had the follow-up in a week, 1, 3 and 6 months. The first study included 21 patients with serious adverse events. The first results showed an overweight loss of 24,4% in six months, without long-term data[14]. The system was redesigned to create overlapping lines of staples, to reduce the incidence of device failures, and a second study with 11 patients showed even more impressive results than the first. In six months, the mean loss of overweight was 46%. A long-term monitoring is needed to determine if there is the dehiscence of stapling line and/or the dilatation of the neostomach [15].

The SafeStitch device (SafeStitch Medical Inc., Miami, Florida) was designed as an endoscopic version of laparoscopic suture, and can also be used to perform endoluminal gastroplasty. This apparatus uses a suction device to mucosectomy, which facilitates the performance of endoluminal sutures to create a gastric pouch, excluding mucosa of suture line. Clinical trials began in 2009.

Several other devices have been developed, and they may have applications for endoluminal restrictive procedures. The Medical Power (Power Medical Interventions, Inc., Langhorne, Pa.) has launched a transoral stapling device that can perform an endoluminal stapling. The endoscopic suture device (Wilson-Cook Medical, Winston-Salem, North Carolina) may also be applied to a restrictive endoluminal technique. While these devices have not been studied specifically in endoluminal restrictive procedures, they may have some potential for the study of transoral restrictive procedures to treat obesity.

DISABSORPTIVE ENDOLUMINAL PROCEDURES

Another endoluminal device for weight loss, is the duodenum - jejunal sleeve of deviation (DJBS), developed as EndoBarrier ™ (GI Dynamics, Lexington, Massachusetts). This device is flexible and is placed and removed by endoscopy. The device is opened at both extremities and positioned to implement duodenum and the first portion of the jejunum. The glove allows food to pass, avoiding contact with the duodenum, biliary tract and pancreatic secretions. It is intended to imitate the deviation of the duodenum and proximal jejunum of a gastroplasty in Y de Roux (RYGB). The anchoring system is self-expanding and placed after the duodenal bulb, thus reducing the risk of migration of the anchoring system. To remove the glove, the proximal laces are pulled to the collapse of the anchoring system in a cloak of rescue, which was designed to reduce the risk of injury in the gastrointestinal tract during removal. Besides weight loss, the EndoBarrier ™ may also have value in the control of type II diabetes[16]. The first prospective study, open and in a single center, was carried out by Rodriguez-Grunert et al, which demonstrated the safety of placing 10 sleeves in 12 patients. The sleeve remained in position for 12 weeks, with early removal in two patients due to abdominal pain. The average loss of overweight in 12 weeks was 23,6%, with the minimum loss of 10%. Three of the four diabetic patients included in the study were successfully controlled without medication, with normal fasting glycemia, only 24 hours after implantation. The fourth patient did not show improvement. Two minor injuries from the mucosa of the larynx in the extraction device were reported, as well as some gastrointestinal symptoms in the first two weeks of its placement[17].

A multicenter, randomized and controlled study was initiated in 2008 with 37 patients, 26 of whom had the EndoBarrier ™ (DJBS) implanted, with 11 patients under controlled diet. The mean procedure time was 33 minutes for insertion and 15 minutes for removal. The device was left for 12 weeks, and 4 remained with it beyond this period. Two groups were compared by weight and BMI. After 12 weeks, average of loss of overweight of the sleeve group was 19% compared to 6% in the control group (p <0,001). Eight type II diabetic patients showed a reduction in drug use [18].

Other endoscopic bypass devices include ValenTx (ValenTx, Inc., Hopkins, Minnesota) and BaroSense (Menlo Park, Calif.). These devices were designed for transoral placement for gastric restriction with or without combined devices poorly absorptive for weight loss. Just as happen in many others endoluminal therapies, these devices are at different stages of development and testing.

NEUROLOGICAL AND ELECTRICAL STIMULATION DEVICES

The gastric stimulation showed weight loss in some patients[19]. This system is being developed to be placed by endoscopy or laparoscopy. By laparoscopy, the placement includes a system called Gastric Stimulator Implant (GSI) (Medtronic Transneuronix, Inc., Mount Arlington, New Jersey), it having been created to be more effective than drug therapy for weight loss, therefore really safe and effective for treating obesity[20] and the Tantalus System Meal-Activared Device (MetaCure USA Inc., Orangeburg, New York), being a device placed laparoscopically, based on new technology called Gastric Contractility Modulation (GCM), which provides synchronized electrical signals with the intrinsic electrical activity of the stomach[21].

IntraPace (Mountain View, California) is currently developing a platform for endoscopic placement of a gastric stimulator for the treatment of obesity.

The truncal vagotomy or vagal blockade by laparoscopy has been suggested as a possible method for treating morbid obesity. It was demonstrated that patients with peptic ulcer, temporarily lose weight after gastrectomy and truncal vagotomy[22]. The vagal blockade devices include VBLOC (EnteroMedics, St. Paul, Minnesota) and TEVX (EndoVx, Inc., Napa, California). A multicenter study (EMPOWER) will be performed to evaluate the vagal blockade and weight loss.

PROCEDURES FOR ENDOSCOPIC REVIEW

Revisional bariatric surgery for patients with inadequate weight loss or weight regained is technically complex and it is associated with increased postoperative complications [4-5]. There are few options available to the management of patients with insufficient weight regained or loss in the postoperative gastroplasty, including behavior modification, diet, exercise and medication, and they are often not very effective and they are unable to achieve a proper weight loss, when compared to the loss occurred in the postoperative bariatric surgery[4]. Once the precise mechanisms of action of a successful gastric bypass are not known (contribution of restriction, intestinal bypass, hormonal changes in the intestine), the recovery of the weight of patients is poorly understood. Currently, endoluminal procedures have been developed to increase the restrictive component of the operation. The presumption that weight regain occurs due to bag or stoma dilation is reasonable, but it was not proved in any prospective study of long-term. However, these are the targets for endoluminal therapy, and studies that evaluate these therapies can improve our understanding of the problem.

The reduction in size of the gastro-jejunal anastomosis as well as the size of the neostomach has been tried by endoscopic injection of sclerosing agents. Sclerotherapy was first reported by Spaulding et al[23], using sodium Morrhuato as an agent. The initial report of 20 patients demonstrated that 75% lost weight with an average variation of 9% in weight in six months after sclerotherapy. The average injected volume was 6cc sodium Morrhuato. The most recent publication with more than one year follow up of 32 patients demonstrated a reversal of weight regain 0.36kg/months and weight loss 0.39kg/months. More than a half of patients started losing weight and more than 90% had weight loss or stabilization of it. A limitation of the study was that only 32 of 147 patients were monitored for one year or more[24]. Other studies have reported similar results; Loewen and Barba[25] reported in 71 patients, 30% of which lost and 28% regained weight, but 42% showed no change in their weight. Catalano et al[26] reported a much higher rate of weight loss, averaging 22.3 kg in 28 patients, with higher amounts of Morrhuato injection (mean 14.5 cc). There is a report that a patient in the study needed to dilate a framework of stenosis.

Several devices have been developed to facilitate the review of endoscopic bariatric procedures. The Bard EndoCinch Suturing System (CR Bard, Inc., Murray Hill, New Jersey) was applied in cases of dilatation of the postgastroplasty stoma. Some reports of successful endoscopic stoma reduction have been published using the EndoCinchdevice [27-28]. Again, the low morbidity in relation to the revisional surgery approach is the advantage of the endoscopic approach, and the durability of the procedure remain as an important question. The Bard/Davol conducted a multicenter, randomized, placebo-controlled study (randomized evaluation of endoscopic suture, RESTORE trial) to determine if the reduction of the stoma with EndoCinch device promotes weight loss in patients who had gastric bypass[29].

The G-prox device with Endosurgical Operating System (EOS) (USGI, Inc., San Clemente, Calif.) was used to reduce the stoma and the gastric stump in postoperative gastroplasty in Y de Roux (ROSE). This system involves a platform on the tip of the endoscope with four channels, one for the endoscope itself and three for the operational tools. With the possibility of performing a deep suture, with total thickness, the stoma reduction of this procedure may, eventually, be more durable. However, the platform is complicated to use and requires a dilated gastric stump to accommodate the apparatus. For this reason, the device may be limited to use in patients who have dilated the gastric stump in the postoperative gastroplasty. Herron et al reported the feasibility of this procedure in ex vivo and in vivo of swine models [30]. A series was performed in 21 patients, at a single institution, with regained weight of 59 lb after RYGB was recently presented at the Congress of the SAGES 2009[31]. Twenty of 21 patients were successful in performing and finish the procedure. Reported a reduction in diameter of the stoma, an average of 53%, with an average reduction of 41% of gastric stump. The mean procedure time was 91 minutes, without significant complications. An average of 36% of the weight regained was lost, after the procedure, followed up for 3 months in 15 patients. The endoscopic evaluation of three months, revealed the presence of anchors in their original locations, the preservation of most of the stoma/reduction of the bag, tissue remodeling, and the folds of fibrous tissue. The authors concluded that the EOS may have great potential as a safe and effective method to reduce stoma and gastric stump in post-RYGB.

An experience with a new device called OTSC-Clip was recently published, which was developed for the approximation of tissues through a Nitinol clip. So it is triggered after traction of the gastric tissue by a capsule attached to the tip of the endoscope. The first results described by Heylen are encouraging. So it was used in 94 patients, without complications with one year follow-up the mean BMI after the application of the device decreased from 32,8 to 27,4[32].

The StomaphyX ™ (Endogastric Solutions, Inc., Redmond, Washington) is a tissue approximation device, which has now been used to reduce gastric stump and gastro-jejunal anastomosis in cases of regained weight in the postoperative gastroplasty with stoma dilatation and increased volume of neo stomach. This disposable device uses an "over tube" with a mechanism of gastric tissue fixation through polypropylene fasteners with the H-shaped (Figures 1,2,3 and 4). The ease of the method and low morbidity seems to be the advantages of this procedure. The initial experience in the United States was published in 2010[33]. In 39 patients submitted to the endoluminal reduction of the gastric pouch with this device showed the loss of overweight of 7,4%, 10,6%, 13,2%, 13,2%, 17,0% and 19,5% in two weeks, one month, two months, three months, six months and one year in six patients followed up for 1 year. The authors say these results are consistent with the initial results obtained in Belgium, performed by Himpens et al and that the StomaphyX procedure ™ can be an alternative to conventional surgical treatment, for patients who regained weight in postoperative gastroplasty. An option to use the device and attempt to close the fistula of the gastric stump in postoperative bariatric surgery. Overcash published his experience with good results in two cases[34].

Other companies are developing similar endoluminal devices. The NDO Plicator (NDO Surgical, Inc., Mansfield, Massachusetts) is not available in the market, but may also have applications in patients with regained weight. Current evidence for this device is limited to a few case reports.

Figures 1 and 2 – Before and after - Endoluminal approach for gastric pouch reduction - revisional bariatric procedure

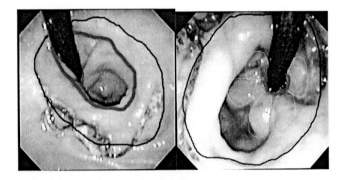

Figures 3 and 4 - Positioning of the team and the surgeon's view

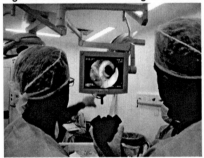

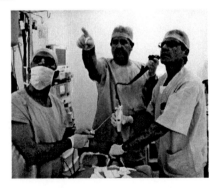

THE FUTURE OF BARIATRIC SURGERY

While most of endoluminal techniques are focused on proving the restrictive and poorly absorbed concepts, our comprehension of the mechanism of weight loss after bariatric surgery continues to expand. With this expansion, appear larger possibilities for the future of bariatric surgery, with they more safe, effective and less costly. Surgical treatment will continue to be important, because of the ineffectiveness of non-surgical treatments for this disease so complex and multi-factorial. The adoption of new technologies for daily practice must be based on efficacy, safety and benefits over the existing procedures.

REFERENCES
1.   Nguyen NT, Root J, Zainabadi K, et al. Accelerated growth of bariatric surgery with the introduction of minimally invasive surgery. Arch Surg. 2005;140:1198–1202.

2.   J. P. Morgan, American Society for Metabolic and Bariatric Surgery, company estimates.

3.   Buchwald H, Avidor Y, Braunwald E, et al. Bariatric surgery: a systematic review and meta-analysis. JAMA. 2004;292:1724–1737.

4.   Schwartz RW, Strodel WE, Simpson WS, et al. Gastric bypass revision: lessons learned from 920 cases. Surgery. 1998;104:806–812.

5.   Jones KB. Revisional bariatric surgery—safe and effective. Obes Surg. 2001;11 : 183–189.

6.   Hogan RB. A double-blind, randomized, sham-controlled trial of the gastric bubble for obesity. Gastrointest Endosc. 1989;35(5):381–385.

7.   Genco A, Bruni T, Doldi SB, et al. BioEnterics Intragastric Balloon: the Italian experience with 2,515 patients. Obes Surg. 2005;15(8):1161–1164.

8.   Awan AN, Swain CP. Endoscopic vertical band gastroplasty with an endoscopic sewing machine. Gastrointest Endosc. 2002;55(2):254–256.

9.   Hu B, Chung SC, Sun LC, et al. Transoral obesity surgery: endoluminal gastroplasty with an endoscopic suture device. Endoscopy. 2005;37(5):411–414.

10.   Mason EE, Printen KJ, Hartford CE, Boyd WE. Optimizing results of gastric bypass. Arch Surg. 1977;112:799–804.

11.   Kantsevoy SV, Jagannath SB, Niiyama H, et al. Endoscopic gastrojejunostomy with survival in a porcine model. Gastrointest Endosc. 2005;62(2):287–292.

12.   Fogel R, De Fogel J, Bonilla Y, De La Fuente R. Clinical experience of transoral suture for an endoluminal vertical gastroplasty: 1-year follow-up in 64 patients. Gastrointest Endosc. 2008;68(1):51–58.

13.   Personal communication, TRIM trial investigators.

14. Devière J, Valdes GO, Herrera LC, et al. Safety, feasibility and weight loss after transoral gastroplasty: first human multicenter study. Surg Endosc. 2008;22:589–598.

15. Moreno C, Closset J, Dugardeyn S, et al. Transoral gastroplasty is safe, feasible, and induces significant weight loss in morbidly obese patients: results of the second human pilot study. Endoscopy. 2008;40:406–413.

16. Rubino F, Forgione A, Cummings DE, et al. The mechanism of diabetes control after gastrointestinal bypass surgery reveals a role of the proximal small intestine in the pathophysiology of type 2 diabetes. Ann Surg. 2006;244(5):741–749.

17. Rodriguez-Grunert L, Galvao Neto MP, Alamo M. First human experience with endoscopically delivered and retrieved duodenal-jejunal bypass sleeve. Surg Obes Relat Dis. 2008;4(1):55–59.

18. Schouten R, Rijs C, Bouvy ND, et al. A multi-center efficacy study of the EndoBarrier for pre-surgical weight loss. Presented at: The International Federation for the Surgery of Obesity XIII World Congress; September 2008; Buenos Aires, Argentina.

19. Cigaina V. Long-term follow-up of gastric stimulation for obesity: the Mestre 8-year experience. Obes Surg. 2004;14 (Suppl 1):S14–22.

20. Shikora SA, Storch K. Implantable gastric stimulation for the treatment of

severe obesity: the American experience. Surg Obes Relat Dis. 2005;1(3):334–342.

21. Sanmiguel CP, Haddad W, Aviv R, et al. The TANTALUS System for obesity: effect on gastric emptying of solids and ghrelin plasma levels. Obes Surg. 2007;17 (11) : 1503–1509.

22. le Roux CW, Neary NM, Halsey TJ, et al. Ghrelin does not stimulate food intake in patients with surgical procedures involving vagotomy. J Clin Endocrinol Metab. 2005;90(8):4521–4524.

23. Spaulding L. Treatment of dilated gastrojejunostomy with sclerotherapy. Obes Surg. 2003;13(2):254–257.

24. Spaulding L, Osler T, Patlak J. Long-term results of sclerotherapy for dilated gastrojejunostomy after gastric bypass. Surg Obes Relat Dis. 2007;3(6):623–626.

25. Loewen M, Barba C. Endoscopic sclerotherapy for dilated gastrojejunostomy of failed gastric bypass. Surg Obes Relat Dis. 2007;4(4):539–542; discussion 542–543.

26. Catalano MF, Rudic G, Anderson AJ, et al. Weight gain after bariatric surgery as a result of a large gastric stoma: endotherapy with sodium morrhuate may prevent the need for surgical revision. Gastrointest Endosc. 2007;66(2):240–245.

27. Schweitzer M. Endoscopic intraluminal suture plication of the gastric pouch and stoma in postoperative Roux-en-Y gastric bypass patients. J Laparoendosc Adv Surg Tech A. 2004;14(4):223–226.

28. Thompson CC, Slattery J, Bundga ME, Lautz DB. Peroral endoscopic reduction of dilated gastrojejunal anastamosis after Roux-en-Y gastric bypass: a possible new option for patients with weight regain. Surg Endosc. 2006;20(11):1744–1748.

29. Personal communication, RESTORE trial investigators.

30. Herron DM, Birkett DH, Thompson CC, et al. Gastric bypass pouch and stoma reduction using a transoral endoscopic anchor placement system: a feasibility study. Surg Endosc. 2008;22(4):1093–1099.

31. Borao FJ, Gorcey SA, Chaump M. Single site series utilizing the Endosurgical Operating System (EOS) for revision of post Roux-en-Y gastric bypass stomal and pouch dilatation. Presented at: 2009 SAGES Meeting, April 23, 2009, Phoenix, AZ.

32. Heylen AMF, Jacobs A, Lybeer M, Prosst RL. The OTSC-Clip in Revisional Endoscopy Against Weight Gain After Bariatric Gastric Bypass Surgery. Obes Surg (published online 03 September 2010).

33. Mikami D, Needleman B, Narula V, Durant J, Melvin SM. Natural orificie

surgery: initial US experience utilizing the StomaphyX device to reduce gastric pouches after Roux-en-Y gastric bypass. Surg Endosc. (2010) 24:223-228.

34. Overcash WT. Natural Orifice Surgery (NOS) Using StomaphyX for repair of Gastric Leaks after Bariatric Revisions. Obes Surg (2008).

ROBOTIC SURGERY - CURRENT STATUS

Ricardo Zugaib Abdalla

Rodrigo Biscuola Garcia

INTRODUCTION

Robotics, as an evolution, came slowly until the surgeon's hands. It has been developed in the laboratory, with the military purpose of operating at a distance, in places where lost the health professional would be a risk to be avoided. With the sponsorship of the American Ministry of Defense and the participation of technological defense centers was created the concept to manipulate a robotic arm in a natural position, intuitive of the operator.

Natural ergonomics associated with vision with three-dimensional sensation and depth of field similar to human eyes and without friction movement of the forceps, as if the hands were in the field. This began in 1991, it was developed in the laboratory until 96, it became commercially viable and in 2000 it was approved by U.S. FDA for commercial use. In terms of manipulation at a distance, it was stuck to the development of telecommunications and efficiency in the speed of data transmission, because the commands and the images must be immediate, without delay or without being at risk of data loss. In addition, the financial investment and the cost of its release depended on its own acceptance by trained professionals and population demand, items that still will appear and develop.

This review aims lead to the knowledge those who work hard at the operative area what had been done, where we are and where this fascinating world will lead us.

ROBOTIC INTERACTION IN SURGICAL ART

With the introduction of robots in the surgical area, in the early 80's, numerous promises have become promising, most of which have not gained importance in regular surgical practice. The advent of minimally invasive surgery led at the same time to the improvement of robotic skills and the emergence of the promising field of training in virtual reality. The investment led to the development of several programs and sets of virtual training and three robotic systems: AESOP®, Zeus® and Da Vinci®. None of them received the robot designation by the FDA (*Food Drugs Administration*) and none is able to perform surgical tasks pre-programmed, which is the official definition of a robot, but new technologies will develop and a new world should open the doors of our surgical reality.

The use of robotics has developed over the past 75 years, but only in the last five years the potential use of so-called mechatronics in the surgical field has drawn the attention of the world scientific community. In recent decades, robots has been presenting prominent place in the area of science fiction, their descriptions vary from machines that monotonously repeated movements, as quoted by Czech writer Capek, in 1921, to the ultra-intelligent robot from Isaac Asimov in the 50's, going to meet the family R2D2 and C3PO from Star Wars and the amazing cyborg of Terminator.

Robots gradually took their place in our world, performing tasks that are repetitive, dangerous or that require great precision, as in the automobile industry or in nuclear tests. While many robots could exceed human performance on specific tasks, none developed intelligence comparable to even a baby with two years old, never showing cognitive skills [1].

Recent concepts of robots surgeon began with the studies by Scott Fisher, from NASA, in the second half of the 80's, whose group has developed in parallel concepts of virtual reality, 3D images and their interfaces[1,2,3,4].

In the throes of the 80s, the parallel development of videosurgery has emerged in the surgical field. Jacques Perissat presented a video of a laparoscopic cholecystectomy in the Congress of U.S. SAGES (Society of American Gastrointestinal Endoscopic Surgeons) causing deep impact on the concept "big surgeons, big incisions". Soon after, Richard Satava and a team of NASA began to develop, under the auspices of the Pentagon military program, a telepresence surgery program by simply summarized by the surgery at a distance [1,5].

In the early 90's, several robotic surgical systems began to be developed, such as RoboDoc ®, capable of performing vascular anastomoses and Artemis ® with remote handling [10].

In 1992, the U.S. military developed the DARPA® program, in order to save soldiers on the battlefield, using high technology. Its use combined remote sensing, robotics, telemedicine and virtual reality, through the use of a military vehicle remote-controlled and equipped with imaging examination of last generation, where, once found the need, the surgical procedures would be started by robotic telesurgery [1,5,6,8].

In 1993, Alberto Roveda performed hepatic biopsy in swine, with the surgical station located in the laboratory of NASA in Pasadena, California, being the animal operated across the Atlantic, in Milan (the delay was 1.2 sec) -, the tactile sensation and the biofeedback were used in this experiment[9,10,11].

The first commercial application of robotics in direct surgical manipulation happened to the AESOP ®, mechanical arm that uses voice commands to control the movement of the optics in videosurgery [5,6,7]. Soon the surgical systems DaVinci ® and Zeus ® (Figures 1, 2, 3 and 4) were developed for commercial use, and in April 1997, it was performed first robotic surgery in patient, in the city of Brussels, by Jacques Himpens and Cardiere[10,11].

Figure 1 – da Vinci Robotics Platform

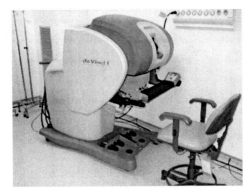

222

Figure 2- manual controls of the robot

Figure 3 – coupling the robot to the trocars to start the surgical procedure.

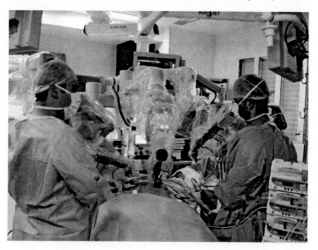

Figure 4 – The robot - assisted surgical procedure

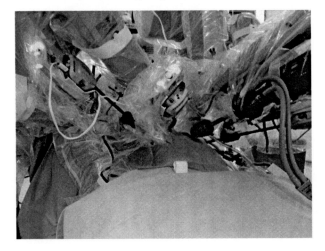

In 2001, the Zeus ® was used in a transatlantic operation between New York and Strasbourg (France), Marescoux and Gagner[9,10] with a delay of 155 msec. It is important to emphasize that delays greater than 200 msec unfeasible the operations made with large distances, because the tissue may move before the surgeon's perception of motion, and may cause inadvertent injuries.

From modalities which best assimilated robotics, urology is the most developed. The knowledge of endoscopic expertise helped them to see better the three dimensional anatomy provided by the optics and dimensional dual monitors, separating the left and right eyes, and restoring the image on the console of the surgeon. The forceps of dissection and apprehension with free movement of seven or eight degrees allowed a meticulous work in small spaces like the male pelvis and complex dissections as the prostate and it related organs. The ergonomic comfort brought to the surgeon is a more favorable point from that surgery that caused tiredness and fatigue of the professional.

Transferring these conditions to other small spaces, such as oral cavity, or other situations that require surgical stability for lymph node dissection in noble areas, we can find advantages and bridging techniques, perhaps, impossible without the robotic arms. Although not

yet widely spread, surgery of the abdominal wall represents a new feasible challenge with the use of the robot, because the articulated arms allow movements previously impossible with the use of laparoscopy or even with the human hand. It is not a new surgical technique, but the use of technology to improve the technical principles of surgery, with benefits, initial favorable to the patient, but extended to improve the surgeon's work.

Many restrictions of minimally invasive surgery prospered due to a difficulty to proliferate, commercially, specific solutions for the improvement of surgical instruments or new devices to aid in the dissection, dieresis or hemostasis. But adding information and medical informatics at the hands of a surgeon comes numerous possibilities that can stimulate a wider applicability with solutions that eventually will be required by institutions and professionals committed to excellence and quality in the best treatment scientifically possible.

The demand for adequate training of the surgeon takes time, availability and, certainly, financial resources. A robotic machine has the ability to work unlimited, depending on the use of forceps of different applications, which are exchanged, or electronically deactivated, after a certain number of use, number, this, safe enough for they do not lose their ideal characteristics of apprehension, dieresis, haemostasis and suture. Surgeons involved in the first training in robotics in Brazil were exposed to the subject at a minimum period of one year, with a minimum period of two days in the laboratory and in some cases submitted to the viewers of the surgery in centers outside the country. All involvement denoted from a dedication greater than the laboratory period with a critical discussion and applicability of the method, in addition to the experience and skill of the group all addicted to medical education and research. The standard training of the notion of technology and how to manipulate the robot. It was clear that the larger the number of people involved, the better are the procedure and patient care. In videosurgery was always required a well trained camera; in robotics it is necessary to a first assistant well trained, an instrumentator; an anesthesiologist, a circulating person among the rooms, an engineer, a computer technician and nursing. Although not manipulate the camera, the first assistant has the responsibility to use laparoscopic forceps to help in the procedure, in addition to meticulous observation of the movements of the robot, which can cause damage to the patient if not properly controlled. The training is similar to all, what changes is the time of formation in each area.

In the first year of use of robot-assisted videosurgery, there have been little more than 300 surgeries in different areas, with their own nuances of services that introduced it in the country, but with favorable results in understanding the use of technology and its assimilation in the healthcare market.

In some specialties, such as Head and Neck Surgery, studies are being performed to prove its commercial viability and its advantage against the costs of conventional surgery.

Because it is a procedure with a minimum aggression, some evidence of shorter hospital stay and shorter time for recovery, better pain control, probably in difficult cases, are already apparent. Due to more extensive training and the need to use delicate instruments, they are exposed to higher quality in the procedure spread to the entire team involved, and perhaps more difficult to demonstrate to the patient who lives the procedure anesthetized.

In difficult tumors, in large lymph node resections and in obese patients with advanced degree it is clear the trends of the use of the method to facilitate the procedure and popularize the quality that the robot allows. In addition, we highlight the ease of working in retroperitoneal pelvic dissection. Who starts with robotics feels an intuitive facilitator advantage, because it is working in a natural position, looking at their own movements in ergonomic shaft.

The intellectual evolution of the robots will allow that parts or all of the surgery will be scheduled previously and performed by them, overcoming the physical human limitations, such as muscle fatigue and our limited articulatory movements.

The decrease in equipment size and its cost and nanotechnology, making small robots working inside our body, should further revolutionize medicine in times to come.

It should be emphasized that the experience that we live in our institutions, allows us to see the difference and the importance that it is combining what is known of the complex open surgery, from a surgeon with experience in the modality, with training in virtual lab, from who is skilled in videosurgery. The advantage is to the patient, the experiments are complete and the result is fascinating.

Robotics and its interaction with medical procedures came to establish itself and grow. Its domain will make of the surgery a better and more complete art.

REFERENCES

1. Satava RM. Robotics, telepresence and virtual reality: a critical analysis of the future of surgery. Minimally Invasive Therapy.1992;1:357-63.

2. Soler L, Ayach N, Nicolau S, Pennec X, Forest C, Delingette H, Mutter D, Marescoux J. Virtual reality, augmented reality and robotics in digestive surgery. World Scientific Publisher Edition. 2004; pp476-484.

3. Gutt CN, Oniu T, Mehrabi A, Kashfi A, Schemmer P, Buchler MW. Robot-assited abdominal surgery. Br J Surg 2004.91:1390-1397.

4. Giulianotti PC, Coratti A, Angelini M. Robotics in general surgery: personal experience in a large community hospital. Arch Surg. 2003; 138:777-784.

5. Satava RM. Virtual reality and telepresence for military medicine.Comput Biol Med.1995;2:229-36.

6. Satava RM. Surgical robotics: the early chronicles: a personal historic perspectives. Surg Laparosc Endosc Perc Tech. 2002;12: 6-16.

7.Wang Y, Sackier J. Robotically enhanced surgery: from concept to development. Surg. Endosc.1994;8:63-66.

8.Wickham JEA. Future developments of minimally invasive therapy. Brit Med. J.1995;308 -193-6.

9.Himpens J, Leman G, Cardiere, GB. Telesurgical laparoscopic cholecystectomy. Surg Endosc.1998;12:1091.

10. Marescoux J, Leroy J, Gagner M, Rubino F, Mutter D, Vix M, Butner SE, Smith MK. Transatlantic robot-assisted telesurgery. Nature. 2001; 413:379-80.

11. Anvari M, McKinley C, Stein H. Establishment of the world's first telerobotic remote surgical service. Ann Surg. 2005;241:460-4.

VIRTUAL REALITY AND EDUCATION IN VIDEOSURGERY

James Skinovsky

Sérgio Roll

INTRODUCTION

Minimally Invasive Surgery, Telesurgery, Robotics and Virtual Reality, these technological frontiers have revolutionized surgical practice nowadays. Every new technology aimed to improve the quality of service to our patients, but the demand of the medical class, the output of scientific inertia, training, spending time,money and stress. Surgeons in the past has led great medical revolutions, such as the introduction of antisepsis by Semelweiss, the use of anesthesia by Warren, antibiotic therapy, transplants and the beginning of minimally invasive surgery by Mouret and Perissatt. Are we on the threshold of a new revolution which combine minimal access, computing, robotics and teletransmission? The advent of minimally invasive surgery led to the appearance of several parallel technologies such as virtual reality and its application in surgical teaching, robotics in surgery, telemedicine and teaching at a distance, all of them with promising practical application. A new world should open at the doors of our surgical reality. This chapter aims to lead to the knowledge of those who work hard at the operative area has been done, where we are and where this fascinating virtual world will bring us.

VIRTUAL REALITY AND THE OPERATIVE ART

Virtual Reality (VR) is a computer-generated technology that provides information with the aim of simulate life in their natural environment.

Although it sounds to our ears like a science fiction movie, this technology is already around us for several years, since the 40's, simulation programs have been used by evaluating and certifying pilots, military and commercial. During the last few years, the VR has advanced to the field of medicine, promising to become in times to come, the next big revolution in medical education. The first movements towards the implementation of the virtual world in the surgical field occurred in the first half of the 90's, already

230

announced by the prophet of medical technology, Richard Satava, in his study *"Robotics, telepresence and virtual reality: a critical analysis of the future of surgery"*[1], published in 1992.

In surgical training, due to juridical problems, the learners are in short supply of operations for training, leading to poor practice and the drop in self-confidence. With the increasing degree of difficulty of the surgical procedures offered in the modern world, it becomes imperative that learners have an arena for their improvement, with the advent of this technology, it became a reality.

Several studies around the globe has demonstrated that the skills to be acquired by surgeons which start in videosurgery are learned more quickly with the use of surgical simulators, besides the exhaustive repetition, because, besides the trainees are evaluated by the own program, making the imperfections to be recognized and corrected effectively [2-11].

Current simulators already allow the trainee to experience the tactile sensation of individualized tissue, called *biofeedback*, the simulation even closer to reality [10,12].

CURRENT APPLICATIONS OF VIRTUAL REALITY IN SURGERY

• Learning in virtual anatomical models;

• Simulation in surgical training: the first application of this technology in videolaparoscopic surgery was in training model for cholecystectomy, and since then several models of sets of training and tasks were being offered, discussed and evaluated.

They already exist simulators in the market for:

- Orthopedic surgeries (Hippocrates Project); several endoscopic procedures involving vascular surgery, urology and digestive tract (high

231

and low digestive endoscopy - diagnostic and therapeutic, endoscopic retrograde cholangiopancreatography, coledocoscopy etc.);

- Videolaparoscopic surgery, which simulation includes: basic tasks - sutures, hemostasis, dissection, etc..; Cholecystectomy; gastrofundoplicature;incisional, inguinal hernioplasty, gastropplasty and others [13-16] – Figures 1,2, 3, 4, 5, 6.

Figure 1 – Model of Simulator - DeltaTech ®, Simendo ®,USA.

Figures 2 and 3 - Colonoscopy simulator, Simbionix®,USA

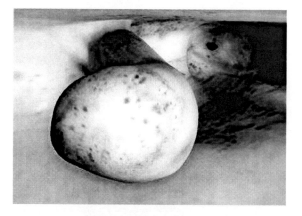

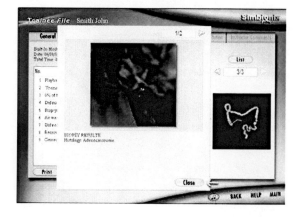

Figures 4, 5 and 6 –Virtual instrumental, Simbionix®, USA.

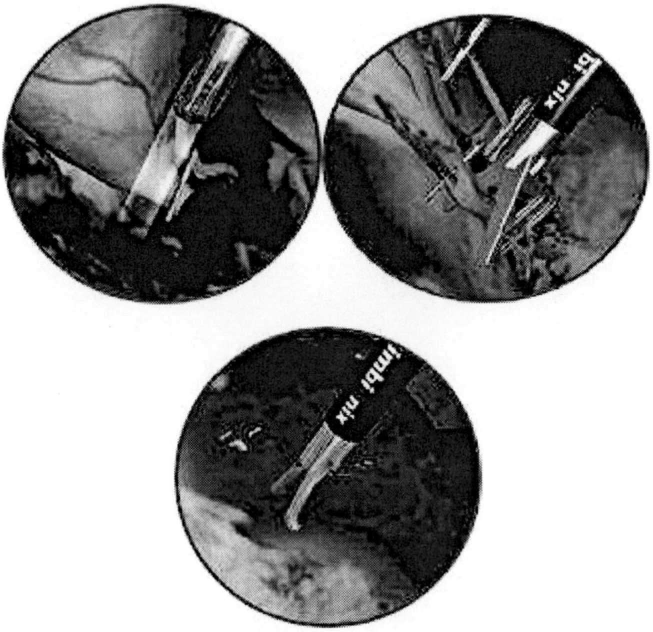

This innovative technology provides marked advantages, such as [17]:

• Efficiency - eliminates the risk of inadvertent injury on real patients, during the course of the initial learning curve, preventing arising law problems;

• Objectivity - the virtual reality can objectively evaluate and measure the technical competence as well as its evolution, even leading to improved surgical self-esteem;

• Ethics - the technique allows initial exhaustive repetition, making the trainee go up the next stairs (animal, human models), now with more safety and skill.

234

• It is less offensive than training in animal models and, may, with the passage of time, become less costly.

• One of its disadvantages is the cost, because new technologies are expensive, but the trend of price reduction caused by competition and technological development is unstoppable.

LOOKING TO THE FUTURE

Like the simulators are now routine training parameters used in the field of aviation and aerospace activity, so also are the medical area. This equipment will allow more instruction on the correct surgical technique without the need of using live patients, at least in the early stages of training.

Like Satava[18] declared "simulators are valid only in the context of a total educational curriculum", ie the simulation is an important part of the learning process as a whole, which should also have practice in black boxes, animals and finally with tutored surgery in humans.

The next generation of virtual images will allow a clear visualization of surgical anatomy in real time, through the interface with individual organic images stored before the surgery, by defining dissection plans according to the internal anatomy of the individual, in three dimensions. It's called Virtual Surgical Navigation.

In 1998, the article titled *"Virtual Reality Applied to Hepatic Surgery Simulation: The Next Revolution"*[19], published in the Annals of Surgery, by Marescoux et al. stated: "Using virtual reality concepts (navigation, interaction and immersion), surgical planning and training, teaching and learning of complex procedures can be fully possible. The ability to practice surgical gesture repeatedly will revolutionize training, and the combination of surgical planning and simulation will improve the efficiency of intervention, leading to the optimum use to the cause of the patient".

Eight years later, in 2006, the "future" was demonstrated by Marescoux, at the X World Congress of Endoscopic Surgery in Berlin.

With the advent of virtual reality, surgeons will have the opportunity to learn and practice the skills inherent in their work area, as often as they want and where they wish, just by a computer program, a screen and a *joystick* game..

The next generation of Internet, with optical fiber 45 Mbyte/sec universally distributed, may become remote surgery a reality in several places on the planet.

Current systems are only the beginning of this revolution, because the near future sees a single workstation, commanded by the surgeon, where pre-operative images of the patient may be accessed during the procedure, allowing the virtual navigation in real time and perfect transoperative anatomical visualization.

In addition, the system controls the environment of the operating room (temperature, light, etc..), the instrumental use and power (cautery, ultrasonic scalpel) and the system of communication with the outside (telemedicine), which we call "Surgical Center of the Future" –Figure 7 and 8.

Figure 7- Model of so-called "Surgical Room of the Future", Sysmatec®,Brazil.

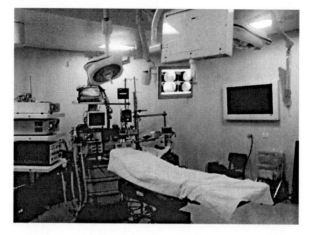

Figure 8 – Control panel of the operating room, Sysmatec®, Brazil.

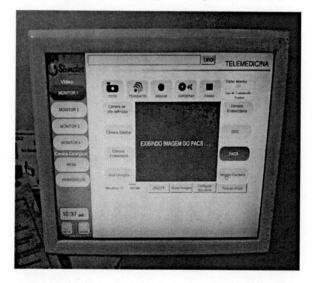

The unlimited human ability to give shape to their dreams, joining the future to the present, to seek the intangible is what gives us the assurance that no dream is impossible and that the time to come actually starts in one minutes.

Welcome to the future!

REFERENCES

1. Satava RM. Robotics, telepresence and virtual reality: a critical analysis of the future of surgery. Minimally Invasive Therapy. 1992;1:357-63.

2. Soler L, Ayach N, Nicolau S, Pennec X, Forest C, Delingette H, Mutter D, Marescoux J. Virtual reality, augmented reality and robotics in digestive surgery. World Scientific Publisher Edition. 2004; pp476-484.

3. Raibert M, PlayterR, Krummel,TM. The use of a virtual reality haptic device in surgical training. Acad Med.1998;73:596-97.

4. Ota D, Loftin B, Saito T, Lea R, Keller J. Virtual reality in surgical education. Comput Bio Med.1995; 25(2):127-137.

5. Ahlberg G, Heikkinen T, Leijonmarck CE, Rutqvist J, Arvidsson D. Does training in a virtual reality simulator improve surgical performance? Surg Endosc.2002;16(1):126-129.

6. Grantcharov TP, Rosenberg J, Pahle E, Funch-Jensen P. Virtual reality computer simulation. Surg Endosc.2001;15(3):242-244.

7. Woodman R. Surgeons should train like pilots. Br Med J.1999; 319:1312.

8. Gallagher AG, McClure N, McGuigan J, Crothers I, Browning J. Virtual reality training in laparoscopic surgery: a preliminary assessment of minimally invasive surgical trainer virtual reality. Endoscopy.1998; 30:617-620.

9. Cushieri A. Visual displays and visual perception in minimal access surgery. Seminars in laparoscopic surgery.1995;2:209-14.

10. Satava RM. Virtual reality and telepresence for military medicine. Comput Biol Med.1995;2:229-36.

11. Wihelm DM, Ogan K, Roehrborn CG, Cadeddu JA, Pearle MS. Assesment of basic endoscopic performance using a virtual reality simulator. J Am Coll Surg. 2002; 195(5):675-681.

12. Wickham JEA. Future developments of minimally invasive therapy. Brit Med. J. 1995;308-193-6.

13. Himpens J, Leman G, Cardiere, GB. Telesurgical laparoscopic cholecystectomy. Surg Endosc.1998;12:1091.

14. Marescoux J, Leroy J, Gagner M, Rubino F, Mutter D, Vix M, Butner SE, Smith MK. Transatlantic robot-assisted telesurgery. Nature. 2001; 413:379-80.

15. Anvari M, McKinley C, Stein H. Establishment of the world's first telerobotic remote surgical service. Ann Surg. 2005;241:460-4.

16. Schout BM, Hendrikx AJM, Scheele F, Bemelmans BHL, Sherpbier AJJ. Validation and implementation of surgical simulators: a critical review of present, past and future. Surg Endosc. 2010;24:536-546.

17. Skinovsky J, Chibata M, Siqueira DE. Realidade virtual e robótica em cirurgia – onde chegamos e para aonde vamos? Rev Cole Bras Cir.2008:35(5):334-337.

18. Satava RM. Surgical education and surgical simulation. World J Surg. 2001;25(11):1484-1489.

19. Marescoux J, Clement JM, Tasseti V, Koehl C, Sotin S, Russier Y, Mutter D, Delingete H, Ayache N. Virtual reality applied to hepatic surgery simulation: the next revolution. Ann Surg. 1998;228:627-34.

TRAINING AND SIMULATION - HOW TO TEACH NEW SURGICAL TECHNOLOGIES

Miguel Prestes Nácul

Marco Cezário de Melo

Marcos Dias Ferreira

241

INTRODUCTION

The history of medicine expresses a constant evolution based on the technical development and application of new technologies, stimulated by the human curiosity and actions of pioneering. It goes back to the ancient age the medical interest for observing inside the human body. In the past, propaedeutics was based solely on physical examination, being the interior of the human body seen only by their natural orifices.

Endoscopy was born with the gynecology, being the vagina the first orifice to be examined through a speculum. In the nineteenth century, different authors had developed creative ways of viewing the urethra, bladder and uterus.

However, just at the beginning of the twentieth century with the use of new equipments and instrumentals, it was possible to access the abdominal cavity with optical instruments, introduced by the vaginal fornix and anterior abdominal wall.

This method, called Coelioscopy or laparoscopy, has evolved significantly over the century, becoming an important diagnostic procedure, especially in gynecology.

Throughout the last century, new technological solutions led to the development of equipment that led to the expanded possibilities of the method from diagnostic to therapeutic. The big explosion of laparoscopic surgery occurred from the late 80's especially the development of micro-cameras and its coupling to the laparoscopic opticsl. In 1985 Eric Mühe, in Boblingen in Germany, and in 1987 Philippe Mouret in Lyon in France, performed the first laparoscopic cholecystectomy.Then settles the conditions that favor the emergence of videolaparoscopic surgery with its fast and dramatic global expansion, thereby giving the greatest advance in surgery in the twentieth century. From this moment, videolaparoscopy was gradually incorporating the treatment of different diseases, achieving the status of "gold standard therapy" in several situations, for example, videolaparoscopic cholecystectomy in the treatment of cholelithiasis. The advent of videolaparoscopic surgery has not only reached the General Surgery and Digestive Tract Surgery, as well as other surgical specialties, featuring the broader concept of videosurgery. The increase in quality and variety of equipment and instrumentals, coupled with the natural evolution of the technical standard of surgeons, led to the fast advancement of the method, which has become highly specialized. Thus, the performance of videosurgery procedures requires a complex and well structured learning process. Videosurgery reached a projection so important in the context of most surgical specialties that the domain of the method has become crucial for the surgeon, including more complex procedures, which determines a growing demand for courses and internships by surgeons from different specialties. Currently, the teaching of this approach is in the center of the discussion on education in surgery. Additonally, the constant technological development has created new procedures such as minilaparoscopy, surgery by single portal or incision (LESS), surgery through access by natural orifices (NOTES) and robotics, which require a greater or lesser degree, of specific training, even if using the environment of videosurgery.

The introduction of a new technique in the treatment of a disease depends initially on its proposal by pioneers surgeons. From this, the technique is accepted by the scientific community, based on methodologically well-conducted studies, which is relatively complex. The comparison of the techniques requires a large sample of patients in each arm of the research, which tends to frustrate this type of study or decrease its level of recommendation. Studies that evaluate specific questions such as, for example, postoperative pain, time to return to the activities and costs have been more used in the comparison of the techniques.

In 1999, Professor Jacques Perissat from the University of Bordeaux in France, described a graph that shows that all "new surgical procedure" goes through a phase of innovation when it is performed by pioneers. Then there is a generalization, to be passing by surgeons specialize in technologically more structured centers and later by general surgeons in smaller centers, reaching a consensus situation. Indications about the use of the technique in treating different diseases are established. Some techniques require adjustments and eventually fall into obsolescence or even in disbelief [1,2,3,5,8,910,11,12,25].

Miguel Pedroso, from São Paulo,Brazil, analyzing the reasons that make the new procedures difficult to popularize, uses the colorectal videosurgery an example. In this process it is necessary to determine the size of the learning curve, what difficulties are found to perform the procedures, the requirements necessary for the surgeon to perform them safely and what its applicability is. Among the factors that hinder the spread of new procedures are those related to the surgical technique, to the patient, to the disease, to the equipment, to the surgical team and even to the surgeon himself. Factors related to the surgical technique include increased operative time and lack of technical systematization. Among the related to the patient, there is a doubt about the benefits, risks of the new technique and unusual types of complications in patients not informed about the procedures. In relation to the disease, they are quoted the applicability of the technique and the small number of cases in which the method will be used initially.

Obviously new procedures require new equipment and instrumentals that generate significant additional costs. In relation to the surgical team, we can see a longer learning curve, the need for motivated teams, as well as resistance to relearn how to operate. The surgeon, often conservative and dogmatic in nature, is facing the situation of having to invest in equipment, training (often long and expensive), sometimes involved in a medical reality with low pay for professionals and without coverage for the use of equipment and instruments needed, both the private health plans and the public health system.

TEACHING OF NEW TECHNOLOGIES

The teaching of videosurgery must be interpreted as the learning of incorporation of technologies. Technological incorporations determine the increase of complexity of the procedures and the performance of new procedures, which determines the need for new learning with the acquisition of other motor skills. Therefore, learning is continuous. The future of videosurgery is related to the implementation of new technologies that cause destabilization in the performance of the surgeon, challenging him to a further step in learning to reinforce their acquired skills, applied to these new situations. In teaching of videosurgery, each new technological deployment requires a specific learning process, requiring proper environment to reproduce this new approach.

The secondary benefits of videosurgery, such as decreased postoperative pain, reduced inflammatory response, immediate return to daily activities, reduction of surgical wound complications (infections and incisional hernia), among others, they were proven and widely retreated in scientific research performed around the world. However, surgeons are always trying to improve the current condition, searching for new procedures to further minimize surgical trauma.

At the beginning of another century, it moves the wheel of history by curiosity and ingenuity of pioneer physicians who will be judged in the future, but, are, no doubt, already part of the history of medicine. With the consent of patients and always in search of a surgical procedure less painful, with faster recovery, better aesthetic results, everyone is behind the "invisible" procedure. As always in the history of surgery, the solution will come through technology associated with medical research. The establishment of these new procedures will depend on overcoming the initial phase of its development. With minimal human experimentation and with respect to ethical guidelines, the pioneers seeking a new level not only for cholecystectomy, but also to any surgery.

According to David Rathner, technologies for the development of surgery in the twenty-first century includes endovascular and endoluminal route access, digital imaging, computer-assisted surgery, image guided surgery (use the browser), percutaneous image-guided surgery, new systems for using energy, molecular biology and genetic engineering (of the tissue). Using the videosurgical environment, they are highlight the procedures through natural orifices (NOTES), surgery by a single access or portal (LESS) and minilaparoscopy. Robotic videosurgery appears with great emphasis, applied to certain procedures and can also provide other platforms applicable to these new techniques [26,27,28,29,30,31,32].

ENDOLUMENAL ACCESS ROUTES – *N.O.T.E.S.*

Also in the area of endoscopy, recent years have shown a change of paradigms, making an eminently diagnostic tool evolved to a highly sophisticated surgical method with an approach, not only of the digestive system, but also of the peritoneal and thoracic cavity. NOTES (*Natural Orifice Transluminal Endoscopic Surgery*) is an extension of the ability of flexible endoscopy to access organs outside the intestinal lumen with diagnosis and treatment objective, including performance of surgical procedures such as appendectomy, cholecystectomy, and others. The idea of access to cavities through natural orifice leads to the convergence among videosurgery, interventional endoscopy and image-guided procedures.

The use of a natural orifice, in order to minimize surgical trauma was first demonstrated in animals in 2004. However, interest in this technique increased after the first case performed in a human being, in India. A new era of minimally invasive surgery could be achieved. The change of paradigm is evident: what was a complication of an endoscopic procedure (violation of an organ) is now considered an access via to the surgery, ie, a common and desirable procedure. Nevertheless, this technique should overcome a number of questions still unanswered. The role of the breach of a healthy viscera (essential to perform the procedure) as well as the possibility of causing serious complications (development of intestinal fistulae, sepsis, etc.). are facts which cannot be neglected, it is being the source of the main question of its introduction in daily practice.

Although still experimental, despite the publication of series in humans, NOTES can complete the evolution of open surgery to videosurgery toward to the scarless surgery, trying to further facilitate patient recovery, probably reducing the need for anesthesia and use of analgesics, as well as improved cosmetic results. The acceptance of patients for these procedures may be higher, which would justify the investment to make this kind of access effective and safe in order to be added to the resources of the surgeon. However, in the process of developing this new method is vital not to repeat the mistakes of the evolutionary process of videosurgery, particularly with regard to education and training.

For any innovative technique to be included in the arsenal of options in endoscopic surgery, studies are needed to prove that it is effective in resolving the disease, with acceptable morbidity and mortality, at least comparable to techniques considered standard. Procedures by translumenal via, performed through natural orifices, reproduce features of minimally invasive techniques by eliminating the possibility of complications in the abdominal wall and obvious aesthetic benefit. However, it remains unclear if its efficacy and safety permit that it can be used on a large scale. Undoubtedly, NOTES represents one more break of paradigms in the surgical procedure, however, it is essential that access through natural orifices proves to be as safe as access through the abdominal wall.

In order to assist and control the evolutionary process of the method, 14 leaders of the *American Society of Gastrointestinal Endoscopy (ASGE)* and from *Society of American Gastrointestinal and Endoscopic Surgeons (SAGES)* met in New York City in July of 2005 to form *NOSCAR (Natural Orifice Surgery Consortium for Assessment and Research)*. Thus forming a group excited by this new modality of operation, but committed to safely develop the introduction of these new technologies. It created a guide to the evolution of the new method, with the suggestion that all operated cases were previously approved by the *IRB (Institutional Review Board)* with recording and subsequent publication of results.

This entity would act, therefore, to coordinate, design and develop comparative studies NOTES x LAPAROSCOPY, realized through government or private funding.

Several potential barriers to the introduction of *NOTES* in clinical practice were raised by the group *NOSCAR* as the issue of access to the peritoneal cavity, the gastric/intestinal closure, infection prevention, development of systems to suture and anastomosis, spatial orientation, development of stable work platforms, training, intraperitoneal hemorrhage control, management of intraperitoneal iatrogenic infections, physiological changes and compartmental syndrome. Another factor discussed is if NOTES should be done by an endoscopist, by videosurgeon or jointly by both. It seems to lack communication channels or information exchange between them. The difficulties in developing the fundamental skills necessary to perform NOTES are evident. Both the NOSCAR created a *"NOTES Team Development Criteria"* that determined clear rules, such as: agreeing to share knowledge, performing procedures on humans only with prior approval of the IRB with obligatory registration of cases, the multidisciplinary team and be a member of SAGES and/or ASGE, in addition to maintaining an appropriate structure to the research and training laboratory.

Among several issues that technically difficult the procedure, the spatial orientation express peculiarities in terms of teaching this new technique. The endoscopist works in line with the image, ie, the instruments pass through the working channels (narrow channels) of the endoscope. Videosurgeon is already used to work in larger spaces, with multiple instruments and access portals with different angles to his viewing angle. The issue of spatial orientation involves using the endoscope in retroflexion, image upside down and mirror image. Thus the spatial orientation can be the main barrier to implement more advanced procedures. Clearly, the experience can overcome spatial inconsistencies, but it is difficult for complex procedures to be performed with the speed and ease of videolaparoscopy, for example. Based on the application of the principles learned in advanced videolaparoscopic operations, orientation and triangulation would be fundamental requirements for all surgical system. However, in relation to *NOTES* procedures, some surgeons and endoscopists advocate the idea that these procedures should be performed with the principles of endoscopy and the use of instruments lined.

As stated previously, another significant issue is to know who will perform the procedure. Who will operate? Jeffrey Ponsky from *Cleveland Clinic Foundation* (Cleveland, OH,USA) already described in the 80's, the *American Board of Surgery* suggested that the resident physician in General Surgery should have experience in minimally invasive surgical procedures including laparoscopy and endoscopy. Remember that many of the endoscopists are clinical gastroenterologists and that NOTES is a surgical procedure and that these differences in specialization and training are ethical, political and economic. Mihir Wagh and Christopher Thompson emphasized that both the training of gastroenterologists and of the surgeons does not involve NOTES and that the management of intra-abdominal complications such as bleeding, perforation, organ damage, is in the field of surgery. The application of *NOTES* procedures in humans will determine the change of training in gastroenterology and surgery. It is necessary to offer advanced training program in *NOTES* focused on the deficiencies of programs of each area. For *NOTES* to mature as a viable technology, technical and technological development must occur. *NOTES* must be performed by a team with skills in advanced therapeutic endoscopy and laparoscopic surgery. At present, the creation of a project that involves these two areas aims to develop the method at an experimental level, to evaluate its potential for use in human patients. The surgeon who works with the digestive system must accumulate experience in endoscopy, including therapeutic endoscopy, which is a challenge for him.

We must remember that the environment to be manipulated in NOTES is different from that experienced by videosurgery, requiring also a specific learning process. As well as in videosurgery, we must learn to operate again! Experimental surgery in animal models has been the foundation for the development of different access techniques for different organs (stomach, colon, vagina, esophagus, bladder) and several performance of surgical procedures (cholecystectomy, splenectomy, pancreatectomy, colectomy, etc.). The use of corpse (*"ELITE"* = *Endoscopic-Laparoscopic Interdisciplinary Training Entity Model*) has also been described. There are inorganic models available, such as the *Erlangen Model*, mannequins, besides the endoscopic simulators. In the medium term, it is also expected the development of specific virtual reality simulators. The NOSCAR emphasized the need for extensive experience with models before application in humans.

Anyway, with regard to *NOTES*, it is too early to establish training routines, these procedures do not have technical or technological standard definition and experience in humans is relatively small. It is necessary to provide cross-training among researchers, encourage the training team for both specialties, developing formal experiences in postgraduate level in laparoscopic and endoscopic imaging[20,21].

SURGERY BY SINGLE PORTAL OR INCISION (LESS)

Starting from the idea established by *NOTES*, ie, minimally invasive procedures performed by single access, using several tools through the same access, it has been proposed a performance for surgery through the abdominal wall with a single access portal or a single incision. Several terms have been used to describe these procedures:*Single Port Surgery*, *Single Incision Surgery* or LESS *Laparo-Endoscopic Single Site Surgery*. These procedures have emerged as a reasonable alternative to laparoscopic procedures, because it reduces the number of access ports and do not have *NOTES* entering through viscera.

They are performed with instruments adapted from videolaparoscopy (normal, smaller gauge or articulated) in a videosurgery environment, thus making it a more pleasing alternative, to the surgeon, facilitating its adaptation for other types of approaches. Some surgeons consider LESS procedures as an intermediate stage between the traditional videosurgery and NOTES, necessary for adequate training and preparing for the exclusively translumenals procedures in the future.

As discussed earlier, the formation of the surgeon to transluminal procedure is more complex, because it is necessary a knowledge and experience in advanced laparoscopy and interventional endoscopy, which is not a current reality of most surgeons. NOTES are used in flexible endoscopy, much more complex to dominate, at least at this stage of the development of instruments.

Definitely, LESS is much closer to the concept of traditional laparoscopy and may be more naturally accepted by the surgeon. Even so, the surgeon needs to develop new skills. LESS presents some peculiarities that increase the complexity of the procedure as the requirement for maximum precision and coordination of movements between the surgeon and auxiliaries, lower range of motion, the difficulty and sometimes impossibility, of maintaining the image of the surgical instruments in the center of the monitor screen, the need for movement the camera together with the instruments which requires movements even more delicate and precise than in laparoscopy. In LESS, the "optimal is enemy of the good", ie, the "camera" is affected by the collision of the instruments that makes the vision often peripheral. However, if the view is considered safe, it is allowed the continuity of the procedure by the impossibility of increasing the visual situation.

The same teaching techniques of the videosurgery are applied to the training in LESS, adapted to the use of articulated instrumental and single portal or incision that limit the range of motion. The use of animal model showed that all procedures proposed are viable. Some factors, however, must be evaluated before choosing the technique of a single incision or single portal to perform the procedure. For example, the use of optical or flexible instrumentation can minimize or even solve the problem of collision between the instruments. The single-incision procedure proved to be less difficult to perform than the procedure for single portal, it allows a wide range of motion, though limited compared to conventional laparoscopic surgery. Whatever the technique, LESS, as well as NOTES, require training as a team, reinforcing the need for adequate training not only of the surgeon but also the entire team. The idea of LESS is not only to bridge the development of transluminal surgery, but also allow that a large number of surgical problems can be solved by this technique.

Only the application of scientific investigation will tell if this approach is superior, or not, to the traditional videolaparoscopic surgery[14,16,24].

MINILAPAROSCOPY

The reduction in diameter of the surgical instruments, for 2 and 3 mm, with the aim of achieving a better aesthetic result and decreased aggression to the abdominal wall, was proposed in the mid-90s by surgeons as Michel Gagner and Peter Goh. However, the low resistance and frequent disruption of available devices contained the initial enthusiasm for its use. With the advancement of technology, this type of instrumental has evolved in its durability and efficiency.

Associated with the development of *NOTES*, there was a real resurgence of the use of minilaparoscopy as a substitute for traditional laparoscopy with the possible use of these devices in other less invasive techniques, such as LESS and NOTES. The idea that these instrumentals have a lifetime much less than the 5 mm ones also has not proved to be true.

With the exception of the 3 mm optical, the other instruments proved almost as durable as the 5 mm.

However, even experienced surgeons may need a period of training and adaptation to migrate to the minilaparoscopic instruments, aiming at an acceptable success rate, with a minimum loss of the instrumental. The pedagogical method to be used in teaching the minilaparoscopy is applied to the same training in videosurgery, adapted to the peculiarities of the most delicate instrumental. Peculiarities of the technique in relation to making knots and sutures and the use of monopolar or bipolar electrosurgery, replacing the use of surgical clips must also be trained in the available models, including experimental surgery on animals[15].

Probably all these different approaches (translumnal, minilaparoscopy and NOTES) act together by increasing the armamentarium of the surgeon for the patients' benefit, assisting in the safe definition of the best approach to be used in each case.

INDIVIDUAL LIMITS AND NEW APPROACHES

James Rosser calls attention to the fact that trainees in videosurgery with previous management of video game, especially the most skilled in these games, perform better in inanimate training.

Selim Dinçler, comparing the learning curve between two surgeons performing the same procedure (rectosigmoidectomy), showed that, despite the number of procedures required to reach the proficiency level has been the same, the surgeons kept surgical times, conversion rates and complications significantly different. Teodor Grantcharov, analyzing 37 surgeons inexperienced in videosurgery, who performed motor training in virtual reality, classified them into four types according to execution time, error rate and economy of movement. Of these, 5.4% showed no improvement with the repetition of 10 similar actions. It seems clear that the learning in the environment of videosurgery brings different problems for each student in dependence, not only of the experience throughout their motor training, from childhood to adulthood, but also the innate and individual potential.

To perform "traditional" videosurgery some adjustments described previously were necessary. Minilaparoscopy requires a little more in their execution, because the basic difference is in handling of a more delicate instrumental. Upon performance of LESS, however, the surgeon loses the important angles in traction and visceral exposure and instrumentation becomes to be held "online", requiring, sometimes, the use of angled or flexible instrumentals.

In Notes, plus handling "online", there is the difficulty of spatial orientation, extremely complicated work in retroversion, when working in a "mirror", beyond the restricted area of handling.

Of these new types of approaches, only robotics represents an advantage for those who perform them with significant decrease of the inherent limitations of videosurgery. Indeed, that's why robotics has had continued fast growth in the last years.

The dissemination and sale of large-scale of this expensive equipment was due to the ease offered to urologists in performing radical prostatectomy in such a way minimally invasive. With robotics, the surgeon who performs videosurgery, begins to have a three-dimensional view with the use of a "*Head Mounted Display*" (the "*Insite Vision System*"), uses a greater degree of freedom of movement due to the "*Endowrist*" system which adds an articulation to the traditional instrumental and, also, allows more precise and more agile movements due to the adjustment of small-scale movements. By the possibility of interposition of a computer between the surgeon and the patient, can eliminate involuntary movements, allowing, in the future, better haptic sensation, an orientation through imaging equipment used as a browser, etc.. It is ergonomically better for the surgeon allowing, also, a tutorial activity at a distance. Despite all these advantages of tele-robotics, for its use, there is a need for additional training, with development of new skills, particularly in the assembly of the robot.

CONCLUSION

Medical progress has been inspired by human curiosity and made possible by the incorporation of technical and technological advances. In recent years, the availability of videosurgery have been widely explored with constant expansion of its frontiers. Surgical procedures considered impossible before, are now conducted routinely. Concepts said as definitive have been overcome.

The evolution of videosurgery was only possible due to the efforts of pioneers both in the medical and technological sphere and the major beneficiary of the application of technological advances is, and always will be, our patient. Because currently almost all surgical procedures can be performed by videosurgery, we must discuss not what we can, but what we must do for this technique. Ivete D'Avila, ex-president of SOBRACIL (Brazilian Society of Laparoscopic Surgery), has already expressed that the videosurgery is the result of the technological development of the end of this century that also fostered scientific and economic globalization. The limitation exists while does not appear technological solution, with the videosurgery only limited by the speed of technological advancement and our imagination. This is demonstrated with the proposal of new techniques such as minilaparoscopy, LESS, NOTES and robotics, which aims to improve the performance of the surgeon generating better results, less physiological repercussion and better aesthetic results, increasing the limits of videosurgery. The speed of new discoveries increases exponentially. Changes determine major changes in pre-existing concepts, but moral and ethical solutions will take decades to be resolved. The reality today shows that videosurgery is not the end of the evolutionary process of the surgery, but the transition between open surgery and the emerging forms of non-invasive procedures.

The central question is how to determine an efficient and complete process of evolution of videosurgery in our environment and how to teach these new techniques. It is evident the need to invest strongly in technology, education, training and qualification. We no longer debate the validity of this pioneering technique, but we worry about how to educate and train residents and surgeons. The use of a pedagogical process more efficient and aligned to contemporary philosophy, which governs the use of videosurgery in the context of surgical specialties, is proving highly necessary. We need more training centers, better equipped, both in terms of human and technological, permanent, with teaching projects of longer duration, with greater emphasis on organizational orientation and tutorial support. The development of "schools that form videosurgeons" must be encouraged. In the next few years, virtual reality and teaching at a distance through tele-medicine should be incorporated into the teaching of videosurgery in a full way. The videosurgery must start already in medical graduation.

The ultimate goal of the educational process is to determine an efficient and complete process of evolution of videosurgery, spreading the knowledge about the method, keeping the gold standard of surgical quality, enabling an effective training and a better structured, updated and secure professional activity. It must confer a solid educational foundation and use modern concepts in harmony with the global trend. It should prepare professionals to develop their evolutionary potential in a "unlimited" way. The improvement of teaching methods and learning of new techniques evolve with the incorporation of new technologies for teaching, where the surgical simulation and full appreciation of the evaluation process will determine a better and faster adaptation in relation to the new techniques and technologies applied to surgery.

REFERENCES

1. Colégio Brasileiro de Experimentação Animal (COBEA) – manual para técnicos em bioterismo. ICB-USP, São Paulo, Winner Graph, 1996.

2. Dent, T. L. - Treinamento, credenciamento e avaliação na cirurgia Laparoscópica. Clin Cir Am Norte, 5:1021-8,1992.

3. Goldenberg, S.; Tonini, K.; Goldenberg, A – A Vídeo-Cirurgia e a cirurgia experimental in Margarido, N.F.; Saad, R. Cecconello, I.; Martins, J.L.; De Paula, R.A.; Soares, L.A. – Vídeo-Cirurgia. C.B.C. São Paulo, Robe Ed., 1994. Tomo I, P.131-8.

4. Ivankovich, A .D.; Miletich,D.J.; Albretcht,R.F.; Heyman,H.J.; Bonnet,R.F.- Cardiovascular Effects Of Intraperitoneal Insufflation With Carbon Dioxide And Nitrous Oxide In The Dog. Anesthesiology. 42:281-7,1975.

5. Kelling,G., Uber Oesophagoskopie, Gastroskopie Und Koelioskopie. Munch Med Wochenschr, 49:21-6,1901.

6. Safran, D.B. & Orlando, R.-Physiologic Effects of Pneumoperitoneum. Am J Surg, 167:281-6,1994.

7. Vitale,G. C.; Sanfilippo,J. S.; Perissat,J.- Laparoscopic Surgery. J. B. Lippincott Co, Philadelphia,1995.

8. Soper NJ, Stockmann PT, Dunnegan DL, et al. Laparoscopic cholecystectomy. The new 'gold standard'? Arch Surg 1992;127:917-921.

9. Keus F, Jong JAF, Gooszen HG, Laarhoven CJHM. Laparoscopic versus open cholecystectomy for patients with symptomatic cholecystolithiasis (Cochrane Review). In: The Cochrane Library, Issue 2, 2008. Oxford: Update Software.

10. Moorthy K, Munz Y, Sarker K, et al. Objective assessment of technical skills in surgery. BMJ 2003; 327: 1032 - 1037.Reznick R. Teaching and testing technical skills.The American Journal of Surgery 1993; 165(3): 358-36.Nuzzo G, et al. Bile Duct Injury During Laparoscopic Cholecystectomy: Results of an Italian National Survey on 56 591 Cholecystectomies.Arch Surg, Oct 2005; 140: 986 – 992 Endoscopy. 2009 May;41(5):395-9.

11. Nácul, MP Rev. de Saúde da UCPEL, Pelotas, v.1, n.2, Jul./Dez. 2007.

12. Marcus Vinicius Dantas de Campos Martins; James Skinovsky; Djalma Ernesto Coelho; Maria Fernanda Torres. SITRACC – Single Trocar Access – a new device for a new surgical approach. Journal of the Brazilian Society of Videosurgery. Vol. 1 - Number 2 - April/June 2008.

13. Carvalho G.L., Silva F.W., Cavalcanti C.H., Albuquerque P.P.C., Araújo D.G., Vilaça T.G., Lacerda C.M. Colecistectomia minilaparoscópica sem utilização de endoclipes: técnica e resultados em 719 casos. rev bras videocir 2007;5(1):5-11.

14. Cavazzola L. Laparoendoscopic Single Site Surgery (LESS) - Is it a bridge to Natural Orifice Translumenal Endoscopic Surgery (NOTES) or the final evolution of minimally invasive surgery? Journal of the Brazilian Society of Videosurgery Year 1 - Vol. 1 - Number 3 - July/September 2008 – editorial

15. Seymour N, Gallagher A, Roman S, O'Brien M, Bansal V, Andersen D, Satava R. Virtual Reality Training Improves Operating Room Performance Results of a Randomized, Double-Blinded StudyAnn Surg. 2002 October; 236(4): 458–464.

16. Satava, RM Virtual reality and telepresence for military medicine Computers in Biology and Medicine. Volume 25, Issue 2, March 1995, Pages 229-236.

17. Satava RM. Emerging Technologies for Surgery in the 21st Century. Arch Surg. 1999; 134:1197-1202.

18. Gillen S, Wilhelm D, Meining A, Fiolka A, Doundoulakis E, Schneider A, von Delius S, Friess H, Feussner H. The "ELITE" model: construct validation of a new training system for natural orifice transluminal

endoscopic surgery (NOTES). Endoscopy. 2009 May;41(5):395-9.

19. B. Hu, S. Chung, L. Sun, K. Kawashima, T. Yamamoto, P. Cotton, C. Gostout, R. Hawes, A. Kalloo, S. Kantsevoy Eagle Claw II: a novel endosuture device that uses a curved needle for major arterial bleeding: a bench study. Gastrointestinal Endoscopy, Volume 62, Issue 2, Pages 266-270.

20. Ali, M, Rasmussen, J; Bhasker, R, Bobby.Teaching robotic surgery: a stepwise approach. Surgical Endoscopy, Volume 21, Number 6, June 2007, pp. 912-915(4).

21. Marecik, S; Prasad, L; Park, J.; Pearl, R.; Evenhouse, R.; Shah, A.; Khan, K; Abcarian, H.A lifelike patient simulator for teaching robotic colorectal surgery: how to acquire skills for robotic rectal dissection. Surgical Endoscopy, Volume 22, Number 8, August 2008 , pp. 1876-1881(6).

22. Muller EM, et al., Training for laparoendoscopic single-site surgery (LESS), International Journal of Surgery(2009), doi:10.1016/j.ijsu.2009.11.003

23. Périssat J, Collet D, Monguillon N. Advances in laparoscopic surgery. Digestion (1998) 59:606-618.

24. Bruce V et Green P. Visual perception: physiology, psychology and ecology. L.E.A.: London; 1985.

25. Perreault J, Cao CGL. Effects o friction of haptic pereption in simulated endoscopic environments. Proceeding of the human factors and ergonomic s society (2004) 48th Annual Meeting

26. Silva JA, Aznar-Casanova JA, Riberior Fo NP et Santillan JE. Acerca da métrica da percepção do espaço visual. On the metric of visual space. Arq Bras Oftalmol (2006) 69(1):127-35.

27. Melo MAC. Questões relacionadas à aprendizagem motora na videocirurgia. Rev Bras Videoc (2007) 5(2):79-89.

28. Rosser JC, Lynch PJ, Cuddihy L, Gentile DA, Klonsky J et Merrell R. The impact of vídeo games on training surgeons in the 21st century. Arch Surg (2007): 142:181-6.

29. Dinçler S, Koller MT, Steurer J, Bachmann LM, Christiem D et Buchmann P. Multidimensional analysis of learning curve in laparoscopic sigmoid resection. Disease Colon Rectum (2003) 46(10):1371-8.

30. Grantcharov TP et Fuch-Jensen P. Can everyone achieve proficiency with laparoscopic technique? Learning curve patterns in technical skills acquisition. Am J Surg (2009).

31. Hu JC, Hevelone ND,Ferreira MD, Lipsitz SR, Choueiri TK, Sanda MG, Earle CC. Patterns of care for radical prostatectomy in the United States from 2003 to 2005.J Urol. 2008. Nov; 180(5):1969-74. Epub 2008 Sep 17.

32. Berry AM, Korkes F,Ferreira MD, Hu JC. Robotic urethrovesical anastomosis: combining running and interrupted sutures. J Endourol. 2008 Sep; 22(9):2127-9.

MEDICAL-SURGICAL TEACHING AND THE INTERNET AGE

Alessandro Brawerman

Eduardo Juliano Alberti

The union of Medicine with new technologies has brought a new world of possibilities. The services offered range from websites specialized in the study and improvement of medical professionals passing through the live broadcasts of surgeries through the Internet, reaching even the most sophisticated solutions such as virtual reality simulators and surgical procedures at a distance, using robots.

This chapter aims to present several possible scenarios linking medicine with the Internet, including concepts and cases of the use of Telemedicine and Internet portals focusing on the study of Medicine and Surgery.

TELEMEDICINE AND CASES OF USE

Telemedicine involves all health services that are affected by the distance between health professionals of the area and patients, or other professionals, and that can be solved through the use of information and communication technologies. The exchange of information provided by the use of such technologies may include diagnostic information, treatment, education or researches.

"Telemedicine is defined as the exchange of information using information and health communication technology and at a distance"[1].

In 2002 the Brazilian Federal Council of Medicine decided considering technological advances, medical needs, applicability of technologies and ease of use, which some medical services could be implemented through Telemedicine observing factors such as: information security, physician's professional responsibility and protection of the patient (the Federal Council of Medicine, 2010)[2,3].

According to the Brazilian Council of Telemedicine and Telehealth, Telemedicine can now be subdivided in the following categories (BCTMH, 2010):

- Teleconsultation - medical consultation at a distance. To this end, may be employed any technological means which carries sound, image or written communication.
- Teleconference - seeking to clarify the diagnosis and therapeutic guidance, by the physician and his patient, a more experienced professional or institution, reachable only by telecommunication.
- Telesurveillance - monitoring of a patient at a distance by a health professional or hospital institution.
- Teleassistance - provide medical aid to a patient at a distance.

A front of technological advances and research that is well known is TEUN (Telemedicine University Network). This initiative of the Ministry of Science and Technology of the Brazilian government consists of an integrated network of universities, hospitals and research centers with the aim of improving technologies and studies about telemedicine. Under the coordination of the National Network of Teaching and Research - NNR - supported by the Financier of Studies and Projects - FINSP - and the Brazilian Association of University Hospitals - Abrahue - TEUN make available to the institutions of the national *backbone* of NNR and community networks, in order to provide infrastructure for communication services (TEUN, 2010)[4].

Telemedicine is already applied in a functional way in several medical services. An example is the telemedicine of Bahia - an institution formed by the union of doctors - which performs transtelephonic electrocardiograms for monitoring cardiac patients, emissions reports of ECG's and teleradiology (Telemedicine of Bahia, 2010)[5].

The transtelephonic monitoring is a registry, activated by the patient, of his heart rhythm. The patient load or use the monitor while is dedicated to his normal activities. The monitor stores portions of the ECG on a digital chip, which can then be transmitted over a telephone line and recorded in the department on paper.

This service is normally provided 24 hours a day, during 7 days of the week and the reports are available on average 5 to 15 minutes after its sent, ensuring exchange of information quickly.

Another example of use of telemedicine was conducted by *Satakunta Central* and *Noormarkku Health Center* hospitals. Located in Finland and 15 km distant from each other, performed a study to evaluate the performed diagnoses using teleconferencing. In the method adopted, a general physician, guided by a surgeon who accompanied him through a videoconferencing, performed physical examinations in 50 female patients, soon after a team performed the same procedures, but in a traditional way.

As a result of this study it was found that from the 50 diagnoses made by teleconference, 48 were confirmed by the traditional method. Patients approved the system because they do not need to go through the discomfort of the journey to a reference center[6]. Can also be added that the system can be applied to areas of difficult access, which is very common in Brazil, in order to increase the number of diagnoses made prematurely.

Professor Genival Veloso de França discusses in his article "Telemedicine: brief ethical and legal considerations" the ethical issue applied to Telemedicine. Genival says that "Telemedicine has potential advantages and its demand will increase as the means of telecommunications become increasingly available and reliable". The doctor-patient relationship is emphasized in the opinion of Genival, because despite all these benefits from the techniques of telemedicine, the principles of credit and respect, privacy and autonomy cannot be overlooked. In addition, the patient must be warned about the risk of remote medical assistance and that although the doctor has his rules of conduct and responsibility related to procedures performed, the patient does not cease to be responsible for any bad results from the use of telemedicine techniques [7].

The creation of new technologies has the progress of communication between people and professions, so professionals can come together - without regard to the distance and without leaving their offices - and discuss about several issues from mutual interest, solve problems or even talk to his patients.

MEDICAL AND EDUCATIONAL PORTALS

In the area of education, similarly, websites offer from search services specialized in the field of medicine, as is the case of Bibliomed, primarily focused on providing learning tools for students and health professionals, to specific guidance to the surgical areas, as is the case of LapSurg and WebSurg whose goal is to provide online training in surgery.

Comprising a team of collaborators from several areas, LapSurg Institute[8] is currently divided into two parts: the portal LapSurg and the LapSurg Institute, presented in Figure 1.

The LapSurg portal aims to the free distribution of knowledge and techniques of videosurgery. There are videos of surgeries, lectures, discussion area and even transmission of surgery on real-time over the Internet, this last is one of the differentials of the portal. Accessing the restricted area the user can consult the collection where can be found articles, lectures, research, interviews and multimedia content.

To complement the LapSurg portal and provide more opportunities for its users Lapsurg Institute was created. This institute aims to offer to the national or international professional, classroom courses and courses at a distance in several areas related to videosurgery and opportunities for programs of Fellowship, in which the professional is mentored for a period of training, perfecting the skills in the newest techniques of videosurgery.

Figure 1 – Lapsurg Institute

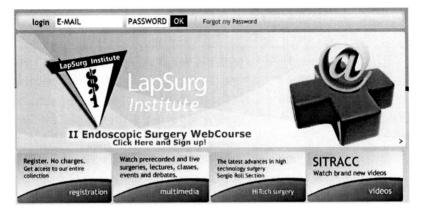

Like Lapsurg, another very accessed worldwide portal is WebSurg - *World Electronic Book of Surgery*. It provides its users with videos of surgery, clinical cases, tips, conferences, debates, interviews with experts and specialized courses. Approaching several areas, the portal is considered one of the largest educational collections of the world on minimally invasive surgery. Professionals who want information can access the link "*Virtual University*" provided by the portal and track the "state of the art" regarding to surgery and surgical equipment [9].

Bibliomed - Bibliomed Internet Company - provides training for all major medical areas. It has offices in Brazil, Argentina and the United States, and it has as founders large health care companies such as *Latin Healthcare Fund* and as partners large medical groups of the host countries. It offers two portals on the Internet: Bibliomed and Good Health.

Bibliomed portal, shown in Figure 3, provides scientific and educational presentations, applications for PDAs, medical articles, Image Base, News, Diet, Toxicology Center and Virtual Conferences. It has, as a large differential, an area where subscribers can consult books and a complete technical section called "Professional Education" which contains links to medical journals, monographs and theses[10].

Figure 2 – Bibliomed Portal

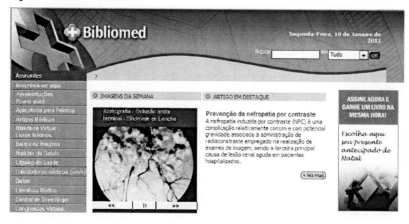

The GoodHealth portal is a Website that provides information to lay users. Approaching in a fast and clear way issues such as routine exams, AIDS, obesity, World Health Day and Cancer. The portal is a good choice for users who want clear doubts of the day to day.

ABC Medicus, with its portal, proposes that an educated patient, based on scientific information, can discuss with his doctor drawing out information more concise and, in some ways, aiding in a quicker diagnosis. The user, when accessing the Website, shown in Figure 4, can watch videos, view photos, check the meaning of scientific names and symptoms in a specialized dictionary, and search by hospitals and physicians[11].

Figure 3 – ABC Medicus.

Another option for medical professionals is The *MedCenter MedScape*, Figure 5. This is an online platform that offers professional content for physicians and others health professionals, in addition to offering education tools. The services offered range from revised technical articles to points of view of professionals and a variety of clinical cases.

The registered user receives personalized information to his profile, students and medical professionals receive scientific information focused on these profiles, while others users are defined as patients, receiving more general and reformulated information, as they do not have detailed knowledge. The professional who accesses his account on the *MedCenter MedScape* Website find detailed information on a glossary with the main procedures and symptoms, conferences, news, clinical cases and expert opinions in several areas and issues (from Health Administration to new treatments)[12].

Figure 4 – MedCenter MedScape

To conclude this section, the portal of EBSCO *Information Services*[13,14] is shown in Figure 6. Through its portal A to Z ®, the subscriber can get any kind of essays, whether articles, theses or monographs, or search for (electronic or not) newspapers and magazines. The Website has more than 81 000 essays sent over 70 years by about 23 countries. When performing a search on the portal the user will get answers from approximately 17 of the most important medical databases available on the Internet.

The professional can also access the link *UpToDate*, available on the user's profile, where he will find answers to his clinical questions. According to the developers themselves, the website has a very simple idea of operating, but unique. The *UpToDate* tool, according to the area of activity of the user, whether patient, physician, educator or representative of an institution, propose to answer questions related to health care of the patient. For this, the website has a teaching staff of experts who provide answers to the questions and provide basic information to understand why the recommendations were made.

Figure 5 – EBSCO.

EBSCO also provides the DynaMed portal, created for physicians. It has approximately 3 000 clinical topics arranged in 36 categories. The Dynamed also differentiates itself from other portals for not offering a direct search to technical articles or books and magazines, the website offers a search to a material summarized and reviewed, as a medical encyclopedia.

RESEARCH AND SCIENTIFIC ESSAY PORTALS

This section aims to present several portals that allow research and provide access to technical and scientific essays to its users.

The UNIFESP - Federal University of Sao Paulo - provides online library from the Department of Informatics in Health, in which the user can search for articles, books and magazines. The library has 514 featured articles, 689 books,

2007 magazines (international), 116 Brazilian magazines and 27 databases to perform the search [15].

Elsevier provides *ScienceDirect* search tool. Through this it is possible to perform searches to articles or pictures that were or were not published in periodicals or books. Its portal has a simplified structure that facilitates the searches in a database and tools that speed up navigation, such as: quick search, historical links and navigation on the home page. *ScienceDirect* has an efficient search engine, returning to the user articles in a classified way, published articles, articles accepted but unpublished, articles with open and paid title [16,17].

In addition to the *ScienceDirect*, Elsevier also provides the *Scirus* portal, online scientific search tool. The website was awarded "Best Specialty Search Engine WebAward" offered by *Web Marketing Association*, which awards Internet portals according to several classifications.

The *Scirus* search portal shows itself as the most complete search site: it has more than 410 millions of technical essays indexed and has approximately 27 repositories. Many of the repositories used by *Scirus* come from universities or research institutions, such as the *Indian Institute of Science* and *CogPrints*. The Website also offers some tools to facilitate the use of search engine, such as: search box for inclusion in *web pages*, toolbar for internet browsers and use a *plugin* for the Firefox browser.

Although complet the portal has a simple interface, very close to that found in general search engines most common, such as Google. The Website has the FAST search technology, provided by Microsoft and used in search services applied to corporations [16,17].

VLH - Virtual Library in Health - is a result of the union between the Ministry of Health, Ministry of Education, Department of Health of the State of Sao Paulo and Federal University of Sao Paulo to Bireme - Specialized Center of the Pan American Health. The VLH offers for free a tool to search information related to the area of health. Its network involves Latin American, Africans and

Europeans countries, networks search such as VLH itself, *ePORTUGUESe*, *GHL* and *SciELO*, covering topics from adolescence to Avian Influenza [18,19].

ProQuest® is a repository of electronic publications. It has a simple and intuitive interface, very similar to the interface of *ScienceDirect* Website. In addition to search its own database, ProQuest performs research on other sites that are content providers. The user can make his search through the search tools: basic, advanced, by topic and by publications. The Website also offers the Thesaurus ProQuest® tool with which the user can enter subjects to search through a list of vocabulary controlled by ProQuest®. The "My Research" tool is an option where the user can save search results, periodicals or other essays during one session or in the user profile. This option makes the search faster when it needs to repeatedly consult works in particular. Another important topic of the tool "My Search" is the creation of bibliographies of marked essays that can be exported, sent via e-mail or made available through web pages, that can be shared or used for further research. The service offered by ProQuest® is paid and back to institutions. Thus the available tools may vary depending on the type of signature [20].

ASTM - *American Society for Testing and Materials* - created by engineers and scientists for over a century, also offers its portal searches, SEDL - *Standards and Engineering Digital Library*. The search portal of ASTM has a different focus of the websites previously described. The website is concerned with providing a search engine focused to the areas of engineering, therefore, materials aimed at Bioengineering and Biomedicine, for example, are easily found.

Professionals who have no knowledge of the technology areas will not enjoy this service satisfactorily, but the website open the doors to those who seek to iterate of research of the area [21].

The IngentaConnect™ is a service, offered by *Publishing Technology*, which seeks to provide visibility to the publications of users that for the first time make available their work online, and offers a search service of excellent quality. For this, the website has an average of approximately 25 million users,

271

a database of more than 13 000 publications, 255 publishers and over 4 millions of articles. The search portal offers free access, but some results can be classified as closed to free reading, requiring the purchase of work to full reading [22].

The Proceed is a Brazilian government program in union with the Ministry of Science and Technology and BIIST - Brazilian Institute of Information in Science and Technology - created in 1995, with the aim of promoting the use and creation of information services in an online way. The program provides methods for organizing and processing information on the web, in order to manage the information needs in science and technology in Brazil. The Proceed maintains collections of electronic documents on specific areas of knowledge. By accessing the Proceed, the user can select topics of interest for search, and can access the Virtual Library from Notable of Science and Technology in Brazil where can be found biographies of the most important Brazilian scientists.

On topics related to biological areas the user will find several items that he can navigate and perform searches about them. Topics are available as experts and researchers, books, articles and other texts, forums, periodicals and others serial publications, postgraduate programs, projects and several programs. Despite not having a totally easy and flexible interface, the website earns positive points for the diversity of content and for its content to be more adapted to the reality of Brazilian professionals[23].

The professional who wishes to seek Brazilian scientific periodicals cannot miss visiting SciELO - Scientifc Electronic Library Online. SciELO is an electronic library composed by a collection of Brazilian scientific periodicals and created by FRSSP - Foundation for Research Support of the State of Sao Paulo - in partnership with BIREME and NCSTD - National Council for Scientific and Technological Development.

The SciELO user can access a wide range of periodicals, and view them fascicle to fascicle, with access to full texts. Periodicals and articles can be classified by subject, author (only for articles) and alphabetical list (only for periodicals) or can be found through the search tool.

The *SciELO* portal also has a page with information and links to evaluate periodicals and procedures for their inclusion in the collection of the website [24].

In order to distribute and promote the distribution of books and periodicals to the physicians, the *Flying Publisher* company developed the Websites: *Freebooks4doctors* and *FreeMedicalJournals.*

Both portals have the same interface and offer the same services, but are focused on the distribution of different materials. The professional can browse through the topics, impact or title of material. If these options are not sufficient to find the desired material, the user may at any time, report the content subject or title of the essay that he is looking for and conduct the search through the search engine on the Website.

The *FreeMedicalJournals* portal has approximately 1 709 periodicals available, while *FreeBooks4Doctors* website has about 365 books (Flying Publisher Books4Doctors, 2010)[25,26].

For professionals seeking to publish and find online publications, the CogPrints is the ideal tool. The portal, developed by the University of Southampton - England - offers the service of "self archiving", ie, the user, by registering, have the opportunity to include his essays in the database of the Website. Can be published on the portal essays that fit into the following classifications: book chapters, conference papers, reports of technical departments, online periodicals or paper publications, magazine articles, theses or other essay. Only registered users can make the publication of files, but membership is free.

CogPrints portal is able to classify the studies published through the year of publication or theme discussed, disengaging the user to use the search engine. If the user wishes to search by a part of the text, title, author or other information contained in the essay in question may use the search tool informing the search that he wants [27].

NCBI - *National Center for Biotechnology Information* - provides to users the PubMed tool. PubMed is a search engine linked to *U.S. National Library of*

Medicine and the National Institutes of Health, has approximately 20 millions of biomedical citations from MedLine, books and online periodicals.

PubMed includes technical essays involving many different areas of medicine such as: Surgery, Taxonomy, Genetics & Medicine, Genes, Genome and Sequencing Analysis [28].

Professionals who want to stay informed can access the periodicals published by medical societies and made available by *SciELO* and also through the sites of the societies.

ONLINE MEDICAL MAGAZINES

This section presents some of the most important and complete medical magazines on the Internet.

The *Index Copernicus Journals* is a search engine, by *the Index Copernicus International*, which provides information about printed or not printed publications. Publications can be found through their titles, areas, ISSN, location or profile.

The website provides information such as: Title, ISSN, Website, publication language, frequency of publication, language of the abstracts and editorial information. It is important to emphasize that the goal of *Index Copernicus* portal is to bring information to the user with which he can access, ask questions or purchase the publications of the magazine and do not provide the publications of it. Similarly, *Index Copernicus International* provides a service of network among scientists, in which researchers and scientists can create profiles and create virtual research groups, enabling communication among them[29].

The professional of the area of Urology can consult UroVirt magazine, the first virtual magazine of Urology of the Latin American. UroVirt is available, online, since 2 006, and has 13 volumes. The magazine is also available through the *Index Copernicus International* portal. The magazine brings to the reader clinical cases and information related to, for example, uropathology, uroncology, urogynecology. It also provides a section where the reader can learn through images resulting from clinical cases [30].

Medical Services is a portal that has aimed to provide information to Brazilian health professionals, update and news of a scientific nature. The website provides to its users online courses, commented medical literature, news, clinical research, medical journals, symposia, lectures and events calendar. The use of the portal is restricted to doctors, academics and health professionals and the information is available only to registered users. Registration can be done for free[31].

"Annals of Internal Medicine" magazine was created over 83 years by the American College of Physicians and is considered one of the 5 magazines with more impact in the area of clinical practice. Its goal is to keep medical professionals, and related areas, informed of important developments in the area of research and development of clinical practice, and assists, directly and indirectly, in the improvement of medical care and the care offered to patients.

The periodical brings to the reader: original articles, reviewed articles, expert advice, public health, policy of health care, medical education, ethics and research methods. The periodical is available in printed format and under ISSN 0003-4819 and in an online version under ISSN 1439-3704. The access to the online magazine is paid, limiting free access to only small versions and abstracts of articles. Currently, access for 1 day costs $ 15, but the website of the magazine offers subscriptions at different prices.

"Annals of Internal Medicine" magazine is a publication of the largest medical specialty organization and second largest medical organization in the United States. It has approximately 129 000 members, including these: internal medical, specialists and students are included [32].

JAMA - *The Journal of The American Medical Association* - is a magazine consolidated in the medical area, published continuously since 1 883 with a frequency of 48 publications per year. In 2009 impact factor reached 28.9, a value calculated through the number of global citations and the total number of citations of the magazine. Approximately only 9% of the articles received by the magazine are published, which shows that the editorial staff is highly critical, maintaining the high quality of the magazine, it also highlights the high number of job submission. Printed publications by JAMA magazine are identified by ISSN 0098-7484 while online publications are identified by the ISSN 1538-3598. Access to the online magazine is partially free, some items are free while original articles and others are paid. JAMA provides access for one day in the amount of $ 30[33].

"*The New England Journal of Medicine*" periodical dedicated to bring the best of research and innovations in the medical area, was created in 1812 driven by the first publication of the first periodical in New England by John Collins Warren.

His publication is present in 177 countries and has approximately 600 000 readers. It is considered the magazine with more quotes in technical essay. The NEJM is the only American periodical to win the *Polk Award* by journalistic merit. Its publications have free access after six months of the official publication for about 100 low-income countries, thereby assisting in the medical development of the country. The editions of the periodical always bring the original and revised articles, as well as descriptions of clinical practice, images of clinical medicine, clinical cases, rescued cases from hospitals, expert opinion and editorial space. Its printed publications are identified by ISSN 0028-4793 and the online publications are identified by ISSN 1533-4406 (NEJM, 2010).

REFERENCES

1. Lima, C. M., Monteiro, A. M., Ribeiro, É. B., Portugal, S. M., Silva, L. S., & João Junior, M. (Setembro/Outubro de 2007). Videoconferências: sistematização e experiências em telemedicina. *Radiologia Brasileira, 40,* pp. 341-344.

2. Conselho Federal de Medicina. (2010). *Portal Médico.* Access in December, 8, 2010:

   http://www.portalmedico.org.br/resolucoes/cfm/2004/1718_2004.htm

3. CRMPR. (2010). *Conselho Regional de Medicina do Estado do Paraná.* Access in october, 12, 2010: www.crmr.org

4. RUTE. (2010). *Rede Universitária de Telemedicina.* Access in December, 8 , 2010: http://rute.rnp.br

5. Telemedicina da Bahia. (2010). *Telemedicina.* Access in December,8 ,2010: http://www.telemedicina.com.br/index.php

6. Pennella, A. D., Schor, P., & Roizenblatt, R. Descrição de uma ferramenta digital e de um ambiente virtual para fins de segunda opinião em oftalmologia. *Arquivos Brasileiros de Oftalmologia, 66,2010.*

7. França, G. V. (2000). Telemedicina: breves considerações ético-legais. *Revista Bioética, 8.*

8. LapSurg Institute. (2010). *LapSurg.* Access in September, 10,2010: http://www.lapsurg.com.br/front/

9. Marescaux, J. (s.d.). *WebSurg.* Access in September, 21, 2010: http://websurg.com/

10. Companhia de Internet Bibliomed. (2010). *Bibliomed.* Access in September,20,2010: http://www.bibliomed.com.br

11. ABC Medicus. (setembro de 2010). *ABC Medicus.* Access in September,20 ,2010: http://www.abcmedicus.com/

12. WebMD. (2010). *MedCenter MedScape.* Access in September,22,2010: www.medcenter.com

13. EBSCO. (2010). *DynaMed.* Access in october,4,2010: http://dynaweb.ebscohost.com

14. EBSCO. (2010). *EBSCO.* Access in October,4,2010: www.ebsco.com

15. UNIFESP. (2010). *Biblioteca - DIS/Unifesp/EPM.* Access in October, 4, 2010: http://www.unifesp.br/dis/bibliotecas/index.php

16. Elsevier. (2010). *ScienceDirect.* Access in October, 4, 2010: www.sciencedirect.com

17. Elsevier. (2010). *Scirus for scientific information only.* Access in October, 12, 2010: www.scirus.com

18. BIREME - OPAS - OMS. (2010). *BVS - Biblioteca Virtual em Saúde.* Access in October,4,2010: http://regional.bvsalud.org

19. BIREME - OPAS - OMS. (2010). *BVS Homeopatia - Biblioteca Virtual em Saúde.* Access in October,2010:

http://homeopatia.bvs.br/html/pt/home.html

20. ProQuest. (2010). *ProQuest.* Access in October,5,2010: www.proquest.com

21. ASTM. (2010). *ASTM SEDL Standards and Engineering Digital Library.* Access in October,5, 2010. ASTM SEDL Standards and Engineering Digital Library: http://www.astm.org/DIGITAL_LIBRARY/index.shtml

22. Publishing Technology. (2010). *IngentaConnect.* Access in Ocotober,5,2010. IngentaConnect: www.ingentaconncet.com

23. IBICT; MCT. (2010). *Prossiga Informação para Gestão de Ciência, Tecnologia e Inovação.* Access in October, 7, 2010: www.prossiga.br

24. FAPESP; CNPq; UNIFESP; BIREME. (2010). *SciELO - Scientific Electronic Library Online.* Access in October, 7, 2010: www.scielo.br

25. Flying Publisher. (2010). *Free Medical Books.* Access in October, 7, 2010: www.freebooks4doctor.com

26. Flying Publisher. (s.d.). *Free Medical Journals.* Access in October, 7, 2010: www.freemedicaljournals.com

27. Eprints - University of Southampton. (2010). *Cogprints.* Access in October, 12, 2010: http://cogprints.org

28. NCBI. (2010). *PubMed.* Access in October, 12, 2010: www.pubmed.gov

29. Index Copernicus International. (2010). *Index Copernicus Journals.* Access in October, 12, 2010: http://journals.indexcopernicus.com

30. Urovirt. (2010). *Revista Virtual de Urologia da América Latina.* Access in October, 12, 2010: www.urovirt.org.br

31. Sanofi Aventis. (2010). *Medical Services.* Access in October , 12, 2010: www.medicalservices.com.br

32. American College of Physicians. (2010). *Annals of Internal Medicine.* Access in October, 15, 2010: http://www.annals.org

33. JAMA. (2010). *Jama, the Journal of the American Medical Association.* Access in October, 15, 2010: http://jama.ama-assn.org/

34. NEJM. (2010). *The New England Journal of Medicine.* Access in October, 15, 2010: http://www.nejm.org/